JOURNEY THROUGH TIME

Journey Through Time

Greta Rose

CONTENTS

1

CHAPTER 1:
INTRODUCTION TO
CHINA'S RICH HISTORY
AN

China is a captivating blend of the ancient and the modern, a nation with a civilization that spans over 5,000 years. This country has deeply influenced global philosophy, education systems, art, architecture, and cuisine. Until the late 16th century, China was a world leader in technology, military power, science, and the arts. While China's burgeoning megacities offer a glimpse into the future, its age-old customs and history provide a guide to the past.

Wandering Through Historical Landscapes

Exploring China means treading the boulevards, riverbanks, and straw-strewn marketplaces once walked by traders, missionaries, monks, and marauders. Each step offers insight into a fascinating blend of East and

West. The ancient beauty of the Great Wall, the glory of the Terracotta Army, and the colossal rock-carved Buddhas and monasteries of Yungang, Longmen, Maiji Grottoes, and Leshan speak volumes of China's illustrious past. For a respite from the global city mayhem, the ancient alleyways in the center of Beijing or the old trading city of Lijiang provide a serene escape.

Leisurely Exploration of a Multifaceted Legacy

To fully appreciate China's profoundly multifaceted legacy, one must engage in leisurely exploration. The past is rich with tales of emperors, concubines, harems, generals, artworks, and silk-clad courtesans. These narratives are compelling, but the true attraction lies in the labor of their hands and the implements of their riches. These relics reveal the nation's ambition, pleasures, faith, and scientific know-how.

A Nation in Pursuit of Greatness

At its core, China remains a nation in enthusiastic pursuit of greatness. This is not just about grandiosity; it is deeply rooted in the belief that ancient principles dictate that there ought to be meaning in every action. Greatness is seen not only as a state of being but as an aspiration to be continually pursued.

2

CHAPTER 2: ANCIENT DYNASTIES AND THEIR LEGACY

Few places in the world boast as rich an ancient heritage as China. The country's history is marked by influential dynasties such as the Shang, the Qin, and the Han, each leaving a profound impact on culture and society.

Shang Dynasty

Our story begins around 1500-1000 B.C. with the Shang Dynasty, which first ruled the Yellow River plain. According to legend, the dynasty was overthrown by a determined and cultured man named Cheng Tang. Made king by the Shang people, he skillfully ruled and eventually revolted against the tyrannical Shang ruler, making himself emperor. Cheng Tang kept noble Shang customs and welcomed wise, talented individuals from all parts of the realm, enabling the nation to prosper and grow strong. Aligned with the virtues of kindness and generosity, his Mandate of Heaven continued for three generations before passing to Emperor Wen Wang, the founder of the next dynasty.

The Shang Dynasty, also known as Yin, is recorded in some of the earliest classical Chinese texts, which are thousands of years old. Carvings in siltstone and bones used during divination processes—achieved by interpreting cracks created by heating oxen scapulae and tortoise plastrons—record names such as Tai, Wu, Li, Yin, and Qi. These bones and shells, one of the most iconic cultural achievements of the Shang Dynasty, are now present in public and private collections around the world. Scholars have debated their importance, considering whether they were diaries, tax records, or the dreams and records of shamans.

One of the guiding animals of the Shang was the black tortoise, depicted on bronze vessels and referred to in records. The history of the Shang Dynasty has potentially woven into ancient Chinese myths, such as the stories of Nüwa, Fuxi, or Yu the Great. Archaeologists today are piecing together the legacy of the Shang Dynasty to understand more about the rulers' use of burials and their relationship with later Chinese culture. One key site familiar to the western public is the Terracotta Army at Xi'an, a representation of the Shang legacy that the First Emperor aspired to emulate and exceed.

Qin Dynasty

Qin Shihuang is an outstanding political figure in history. He ended the state of division under the feudal system, established a centralized country under the control of other regions of the Yellow Emperor, and unified China into a vast territory, profoundly impacting Chinese history.

The Qin Dynasty (221-206 B.C.) saw the construction of the emperor's tomb, estimated to have involved approximately one million men toiling for 16 years. This tomb, guarded by the army of terracotta warriors, included a map, vessels filled with mercury, and even a ceiling of pearls. Chinese civilization had a nearly three-thousand-year history when this tomb was built, marking the end of a long line of societies characterized by decorative bronzes, jade burial suits, vast canal systems, a huge military, and a thriving bureaucracy.

The Qin Dynasty established a national system and a strictly centralized administrative system. Economically, various industries and trades developed well, with copper coins used as currency. In culture, the creation of the Great Wall and vibrant cities symbolized the dynasty's achievements. Although often associated with the Tang and Song dynasties, the prosperity of cities arguably reached its peak during the Qin Dynasty. The creation of the Great Wall significantly raised China's historical profile.

Han Dynasty

The Han Dynasty ruled China from 206 B.C. until A.D. 220, with a brief interruption of around 15 years (A.D. 9-25) by the usurper Wang Mang. Nineteen rulers took the title of emperor under the Han, producing historical records that have come to play a central role in Chinese history. Historians have labeled the subsequent 2,000-year-plus time span as "post-Han." Men and women alive today may still be called Hanren, "people who carry on the Han tradition."

The combined reign of the Western (206 B.C.-A.D. 8) and Eastern (A.D. 23-220) Han Dynasties is considered the golden age of Chinese civilization. Contact with the expanded Western world made many goods from afar available to elite Chinese, stimulating domestic industry. Exposure to new ideas also increased awareness of necessary changes in governmental and social institutions, inspiring the long-lived "New Text" school of Confucianism.

High taxes, initially to pay for political unification and later to finance the military and corrupt government organs, spurred numerous peasant (and at times elite) uprisings. The dynasty came to an end when the last emperor, by then a mere boy, was deposed by his generalissimo.

3

CHAPTER 3: GREAT WALL OF CHINA: ENGINEERING MARVEL

The Great Wall of China was conceived and constructed to keep foreign invaders at bay, protecting various ancient Chinese dynasties with a host of fortifications. Now referred to as the "Northern Wall of the Yang Kingdom" to differentiate it from other sections, the wall served as a significant defense system, guarding the ancient capital of Xian (though it was located roughly 125 miles to the north). Initially constructed as early as 770 B.C., the modern and significantly restored structure was primarily assembled between 1375 and 1368 A.D. by the first Ming Emperor, with work continuing through the Ming Dynasty until 1644.

Spanning Vast Distances

The Great Wall of China spans upwards of 4,000 miles, beginning at the Bo Hai Sea and extending to the frigid Gobi Desert, cutting across Southern Mongolia.

Some researchers estimate the exact length to be closer to 20,000 miles, including a series of parallel structural features such as levees, natural barriers, hills, eroded sections, and more. These features serve as both additional barriers and connections to the main structure.

Construction and Features

The majority of the wall is made of tamped earth and stone, interspersed with watchtowers—tall, dense structures designed to house soldiers, merchandise, and assist with the coordination and management of crews and resources. These watchtowers also served to scare off Mongolian horseback raiders. Today, this incredible structure stands as an architectural marvel, a symbol of historical depth, and an entrance to Chinese culture.

Modern-Day Visits

Today, the Great Wall can be visited at numerous locations, including many renowned landmarks near Beijing such as Badaling and Simatai (which is the most beautiful but currently under renovation). Visitors can marvel at this ancient structure and appreciate its historical significance and engineering prowess.

4

CHAPTER 4: SILK ROAD: TRADE, CULTURE, AND EXCHANGE

The southernmost city within the province of Gansu, Zhangye, is an old town that served as a critical site along the Silk Road. Echoing the city's past role, the culture and ethnic makeup of this area blend peoples who traveled the trade routes connecting East with West. The town of Zhangye is set on the edge of the Gobi Desert and was an especially important regional hub during the Western Han Dynasty. The central portion of this section of the ancient trade route is centered near Jiuquan in the Suzhou District.

Cultural Convergence in Zhangye

The Zhangye section was an integral part of the convergence of the North Silk Road, South Silk Road, and the corridor through the Wei River Basin that linked Przewalski's horses and other Central Asian wonders.

Zhangye was an economic and cultural nexus where East and West met both physically and conceptually.

The Significance of the Silk Road

The Silk Road has been an indispensable lifeline for cultural exchange and economic development between the East and the West. Through discussions and group programs, participants in the flag exhibit at various levels unveiled a number of profound Silk Road sites in both China and other countries. The corridor has seen the most prosperous commercial exchanges, making it a significant route for traders, merchants, and explorers.

Modern Influence and Legacy

By the occasion of the first Chinese Expo, the development of silk and silk culture became an important way to share Chinese culture within China and with the outside world. This historical trade route not only facilitated the exchange of goods but also fostered the transmission of ideas, art, religion, and technology.

5

CHAPTER 5: CHINESE PHILOSOPHY: CONFUCIANISM, TAOIS

Chinese philosophy is one of the most concentrated and direct representations of Chinese heritage. Due to China's geographic location in East Asia, bordered by the Pacific Ocean to the east, the collision and communication between different civilizations have historically been limited. This isolation helped develop three main representative philosophical systems of Chinese tradition: Confucianism, Taoism, and Buddhism. Each system has strong national characteristics and is deeply rooted in the Chinese family structure.

Confucianism

Confucianism, known as the "School of Scholars" or "Orthodoxy" in ancient times, interprets its thoughts as teachable and learnable, and places great importance on politics and ethics. Confucianism was embraced by officials during the Tang, Song, Ming, and Qing Dynasties and significantly contributed to China's society, economy, and culture by promoting economic development and modernization. The philosophy focuses on humanity, with benevolence as the love of God, and advocates for rulers to lead with virtue.

Confucianism's emphasis on moral values, filial piety, and social harmony has resonated with people beyond China's borders. Currently, more and more people in China, the Asia-Pacific region, the United States, and elsewhere are studying Chinese Confucian thought. This resurgence highlights Confucianism's enduring influence and relevance in modern society.

Taoism

Taoism, also known as "Chinese law," centers on the concept of "the Tao," which is often described as an indescribable force or path. The foundational belief in Taoism is that the Tao "cannot be spoken of" and that "go is not the Tao." Taoism emphasizes living in harmony with nature and the universe.

From a human perspective, Taoism underscores the profound and the immortality of people. It teaches that by aligning with the natural order and embracing simplicity, individuals can achieve a state of balance and tranquility. Taoist practices, such as meditation and Tai Chi, aim to cultivate inner peace and spiritual enlightenment.

Buddhism

Buddhism, originating from ancient India, is both a religious and philosophical system. It encompasses ultimate truths of practice and aims for the propagation and salvation of all mankind. Buddhism was introduced to China around the 1st century A.D. and has since become deeply integrated into Chinese culture and philosophy.

The three philosophical systems—Confucianism, Taoism, and Buddhism—have significantly influenced China's national culture and philosophy. They represent the wisdom and depth of Chinese philosophical thought and continue to shape Chinese society today.

6

CHAPTER 6: TRADITIONAL CHINESE MEDICINE: PRINCIPLE

The Chinese civilization is one of the oldest, richest, and most enduring on the planet, renowned for many remarkable ancient achievements. Among these achievements is the tradition of Chinese medicine, a unique corpus of medical knowledge and practice that has been distinct through millennia. This local medicine is distinguished not only by its practices, such as the use of herbal medications and moxibustion, but also by its philosophical background, which contrasts with what is now known in societal reports as 'biomedicine' by emphasizing holistic and energy-based approaches.

Principles of Qi and Balance

The principle of Qi and balance is essential to an understanding of Chinese medicine and cannot be easily conveyed. In essence, the theory holds that the body is a complex network of organs, channels, and systems.

Health is viewed as a manifestation of an energetic equilibrium among these components, whereas illness results from breakdowns in this equilibrium. Traditional Chinese Medicine (TCM) offers a wealth of practical advice alongside this esoteric understanding of health and illness.

Practical Applications

TCM provides dietary advice, exercises, and lifestyle strategies, all aimed at helping individuals regain or preserve harmony and health. The approach to diagnosis and therapy involves a detailed examination of many different aspects of a patient's condition, focusing on core principles such as:

1. **Holistic Health**: TCM emphasizes the interconnectedness of the body, mind, and environment. Treatments often include herbal remedies, acupuncture, and qigong, which aim to restore balance and promote overall well-being.
2. **Preventive Care**: TCM places a strong emphasis on preventing illness through maintaining balance and harmony. Regular practices such as tai chi and dietary adjustments are encouraged to enhance health and prevent disease.
3. **Personalized Treatment**: Each patient is unique, and TCM practitioners tailor treatments to the individual's specific condition, considering factors like age, lifestyle, and underlying health issues.

Key Practices

· **Herbal Medicine**: The use of herbs is a cornerstone of TCM, with thousands of plants, minerals, and animal products used to create remedies aimed at restoring balance and health.

· **Acupuncture**: This practice involves inserting fine needles into specific points on the body to stimulate Qi flow and promote healing.

· **Moxibustion**: This technique involves burning dried mugwort on specific points of the body to stimulate circulation and enhance the flow of Qi.

· **Qigong**: A practice combining movement, meditation, and controlled breathing to enhance physical and mental health by cultivating and balancing Qi.

7

CHAPTER 7: CHINESE CALLIGRAPHY AND ARTISTIC TRADIT

Despite its breakneck pace in technological advancement, China remains a land of ancient treasures and rich cultural history. Chinese calligraphy and artistic traditions have roots that extend back to ancient times, and contemporary China continues to celebrate and carry on these unique traditions. Visitors may delight in stumbling across an artisan painting calligraphy on a busy side street or discovering a public space showcasing a traditional art installation. These diverse works of art are not solely for aesthetics but also serve as a cultural reflection of the collective identity of citizens from hundreds and thousands of years ago.

Calligraphy: The Art of Writing

Calligraphy is one of China's most well-known art forms. Known as Shufa, the term translates to "lines of writing" or, in more academic applications, Guifa, meaning "ancient writing." Calligraphy first appeared in the late Neolithic period and has since played various essential roles within Chinese culture.

The key to attaining self-discipline is calligraphy, defined as the sophistication of the most essential form of internal beauty. In China, calligraphy is greatly valued not only for its aesthetic qualities but also for its moral implications. It is considered one of the most important fine art forms, reflecting the deep connection between beauty and virtue in Chinese culture.

The Significance of Artistic Traditions

Chinese culture is heavily influenced by both aesthetics and morals, and artistic traditions are interwoven with cultural and ethical values. These traditions encompass a wide range of art forms, including painting, sculpture, ceramics, and more.

- **Painting**: Traditional Chinese painting often depicts landscapes, flora, and fauna, using techniques that emphasize brushwork and the harmonious use of color.
- **Sculpture**: Ancient Chinese sculptures, ranging from intricate jade carvings to grand Buddhist statues, reflect the skill and creativity of Chinese artisans.
- **Ceramics**: Chinese ceramics, such as porcelain and pottery, are renowned for their craftsmanship and beauty, with pieces often reflecting the cultural and historical context in which they were created.

Modern Celebrations of Tradition

Contemporary China continues to celebrate and preserve these artistic traditions. Public spaces, museums, and cultural festivals often showcase traditional arts, allowing both locals and visitors to appreciate the rich heritage. Artisans and artists continue to practice and innovate within these traditions, ensuring their relevance and vibrancy in the modern world.

8

CHAPTER 8: MODERN CHINA: ECONOMIC GROWTH AND TECHN

China has experienced a remarkable wave of economic growth over the past few decades. The people of China have made significant sacrifices to achieve this, but now they are beginning to reap the benefits. My journey took me not only through China's magnificent landscapes and monumental achievements in ancient history but also through the astonishing new face of China's cities, which are hotbeds of modern technological innovations. Today, marvels of modern China include the new Three Gorges Dam, the longest sea-crossing bridge in the world, the world's fastest trains, the soon-to-be-world's-tallest-building, and many other supertall skyscrapers with designs that would have been impossible in earlier times.

Architectural and Engineering Wonders

The architectural and engineering wonders of modern China are impressive, though not universally admired. Western commentators often decry the cruelty, waste, and ecological destruction these structures represent. Despite this, they stand as symbols of China's rapid progress and ambitious future.

- **Three Gorges Dam**: This colossal dam on the Yangtze River is the world's largest power station in terms of installed capacity and has significantly influenced flood control and river navigation.
- **Longest Sea-Crossing Bridge**: The Hong Kong-Zhuhai-Macao Bridge, spanning 55 kilometers (34 miles), is an engineering marvel connecting Hong Kong, Zhuhai, and Macao across the Pearl River Delta.
- **World's Fastest Trains**: China's high-speed rail network is the largest in the world, with trains reaching speeds of up to 350 km/h (217 mph), reducing travel times across vast distances.
- **Supertall Skyscrapers**: Cities like Shanghai, Shenzhen, and Beijing are home to some of the tallest buildings in the world, showcasing cutting-edge architectural designs.

Bridging Ancient and Modern

Unfortunately, what lies between China's towering achievements of ancient history and the newest wonders of the modern age is too often overlooked. In this record of my journey through China, I aim to fill in this gap. This led to an itinerary that took me far off the beaten path for Western tourists in China. For the first week of the journey, I passed through the great urban centers from Beijing to Nanjing, with a short detour into Hebei to visit the old Longxing Si pagoda in Zhengding, one of the earliest wooden buildings in China. With this long stretch in China's cities behind me, the remainder of the itinerary was almost exclusively rural.

Rural Exploration

Venturing into the rural areas of China revealed a different side of the country, where traditional lifestyles and landscapes coexist with modern advancements. These regions offer a unique perspective on China's development, highlighting the contrasts and continuities that define the nation's journey.

9

CHAPTER 9: MEGA-CITIES AND URBANIZATION IN CHINA

In the late 1980s, Deng Xiaoping pioneered the policy of moving 300 million peasants out of the rustbelt countryside and into booming towns. As a result, China today is 60-70 percent urban, boasting the largest reservoir of urban dwellers on the planet. In addition, one-sixth of the national GDP is poured into urban development, leading to the creation of mega-cities such as Shanghai, whose home population of 16 million doubles during the workweek, and Beijing, located in the middle of the Chinese landmass, where 19 million people arrive by trains, planes, and automobiles daily.

Urbanization and Economic Development

Supporting "urbanization" on this scale was arguably the basis for the gigantic Three Gorges Dam built on the Yangtze River. The goal, according to colonial dis-course and rural-urban migrant conversations, is to "es-cape from poverty." Upon arrival, many migrants establish family-run terraced sidewalk enterprises, known as "sidewalker capitalism." However, life in the city is known to be harder than in the countryside. In the congestion of city streets, pedestrians carrying gro-ceries home on their bikes often get squeezed out by ve-hicles.

Urbanization: More Than Physical Structures

On closer analysis, urbanization is not just about physical structures and human movements; it is a cul-tural phenomenon that is reshaping who we are and how we think and behave. This massive shift to urban living has profound implications for Chinese society, culture, and the daily lives of its people.

- **Economic Opportunities and Challenges**: Urbanization has created new economic opportu-nities, but it also brings challenges, such as income inequality, housing shortages, and environmental degradation.
- **Cultural Shifts**: The influx of rural populations into urban centers has led to significant cultural shifts, blending traditional rural lifestyles with modern urban sensibilities. This fusion is evident in the vibrant street markets, local cuisines, and evolving social norms.
- **Infrastructure Development**: The rapid ex-pansion of cities necessitates extensive infrastruc-ture development, from transportation networks

to public services, to accommodate the growing urban population.

10

CHAPTER 10: CHINESE CUISINE: REGIONAL VARIETIES AN

Food is deeply pivotal to Chinese culture, making China one of the few countries in the world that can claim not just one national cuisine but many. Each province features the regional delicacies of its inhabitants, and these local cuisines are not uniformly Chinese. Many provinces in China are home to hundreds of thousands of non-Han Chinese, who have preserved their own styles of cooking while assimilating to modernity in other ways. Similarly, many countries have Chinatowns where Chinese immigrants continue to cook traditional food, mainly Cantonese or Hakka cuisine from the Guangdong or Fujian provinces. As the Chinese themselves say, if you want to eat Sichuan food, you should go to Sichuan.

Regional Varieties and Culinary Heritage

An immigrant population's food often accurately reflects their national culture and intelligence, and this is true for Chinese cuisine. Everywhere in China, the tastes and textures of dishes reflect the agricultural bounty of the region. From the mountain plateaus of Yunnan province to the seaside cities of the east coast, both typical and new eats can be enjoyed. The Chinese are famous as food lovers, but vegetarians and animal welfare proponents should exercise caution. In a country of 1.3 billion, someone has likely eaten it and possesses an untranslatable love for it. Since China is both a huge culinary nation and less than 0.1% of the population is vegetarian, asking for vegetarian food in most places, even expensive restaurants, is inadvisable.

Major Regional Cuisines

1. **Sichuan Cuisine**: Known for its bold flavors, particularly the use of garlic and chili peppers, as well as the unique flavor of Sichuan peppercorns, which create a numbing sensation.
2. **Cantonese Cuisine**: Emphasizes fresh ingredients, mild flavors, and a wide variety of seafood. Dim sum, a collection of small dishes, is a hallmark of Cantonese cuisine.
3. **Hunan Cuisine**: Features spicy and sour flavors with a liberal use of chili peppers, garlic, and shallots. Known for its rich and hearty dishes.
4. **Shandong Cuisine**: Characterized by its use of seafood, poultry, and clear broths. This cuisine is noted for its emphasis on freshness and tenderness.

5. **Jiangsu Cuisine**: Focuses on fresh ingredients with a balance of sweet and salty flavors. Famous for its elaborate presentations and careful preparation techniques.
6. **Fujian Cuisine**: Known for its umami flavors, particularly those derived from seafood and woodland delicacies like mushrooms and bamboo shoots.
7. **Zhejiang Cuisine**: Emphasizes fresh and delicate flavors with a variety of seafood dishes. The food is often light, fresh, and crispy.
8. **Anhui Cuisine**: Known for its use of wild herbs and strong flavors, often featuring stewed and braised dishes.

Contemporary Influences

Chinese cuisine continues to evolve, influenced by modern culinary trends and global exchange. Traditional techniques are being reinterpreted, and new dishes are being created, reflecting China's dynamic food culture. Food remains a central part of social life and cultural identity in China, celebrated in festivals, family gatherings, and everyday meals.

11

CHAPTER 11: CHINESE FESTIVALS AND CELEBRATIONS

Festivals and celebrations hold great importance in Chinese culture. The Chinese calendar is a traditional lunisolar calendar, so the exact dates of traditional festivals change from year to year. Here are 11 of the most important festivals in China, listed in order of their occurrence throughout the year:

Chinese New Year (◇◇, chūn jié) - February

The Spring Festival, or Chinese New Year, is the most important time for family reunions. It marks the beginning of the lunar new year and is celebrated with lavish meals, fireworks, and the exchange of red envelopes (hongbao) filled with money for good luck.

National Day (◇◇◇, guó qìng jié) - October

National Day commemorates the founding of the People's Republic of China in 1949. It is celebrated with grand parades, fireworks, and various festivities across the country.

Children's Day – June 1

Children's Day is celebrated on June 1 each year. It is a time to give extra attention to children in one's family, neighborhood, or village. Parties, special outings, and gifts are common, and the day also serves as a reminder and support for children's rights.

Tomb-Sweeping Day (◇◇◇, qīng míng jié) – March or April

The Tomb-Sweeping Day, also known as Qingming, is a time for people to honor their ancestors by sweeping their tombs and offering sacrifices. Many also enjoy a day out in the countryside. This tradition is similar to visiting cemeteries on Memorial or Veterans Days in other countries.

Labor Day (◇◇◇, láo dòng jié) – May 1

Labor Day is a significant holiday for the workers of China. Celebrated on May 1, it is a day for recognizing the contributions of workers. Special treatment and celebrations are common for young people on this day.

Dragon Boat Festival (◇◇◇, duān wǔ jié) – June

The Dragon Boat Festival, also called the Double Fifth Festival, is celebrated on the fifth day of the fifth lunar month. It commemorates Qu Yuan, a poet-statesman who drowned himself in protest against the emperor's corruption. The festival is marked by dragon boat races and the eating of zongzi (sticky rice dumplings).

Mid-Autumn Festival (◇◇◇, zhōng qiū jié) – August-September

The Mid-Autumn Festival is one of the most romanticized Chinese festivals. It is celebrated with mooncakes, a delicacy made with a thin pastry skin and various fillings like red bean paste, lotus seed paste, or salted egg yolk. The festival celebrates the harvest and the full moon, symbolizing unity and togetherness.

12

CHAPTER 12: ENVIRONMENTAL CHALLENGES AND CONSERVAT

The environmental challenge in China is vast. The country's tumultuous industrialization, combined with rapid urbanization and an ever-growing population, has put immense pressure on the local landscape. While pollution problems attract the bulk of reporting, on-the-ground environmental conservation efforts paint a different picture—one that aligns more closely with global conservation projects. However, there is a disconnect between Western and local views of China's environment and the state of its protected areas. While Western publications often highlight a lack of finances for Chinese forestry bureaus and their inability to manage parks effectively, an increasing number of local Chinese researchers strongly believe in China's protected area network.

The Environmental Impact of Rapid Development

China's rapid industrialization and urbanization have led to significant environmental degradation, including air and water pollution, deforestation, and loss of biodiversity. The focus on economic growth has often overshadowed environmental concerns, leading to severe ecological consequences.

Conservation Efforts and Protected Areas

Despite these challenges, China has made strides in environmental conservation. The country has established numerous protected areas and national parks to preserve its natural heritage and biodiversity. Local researchers and conservationists are working tirelessly to manage and protect these areas effectively, often collaborating with international organizations.

Ecotourism and Community Involvement

In many cases, the environment—and the species within it—serves as a main attraction for tourists. Despite their reputation for environmental degradation, there is potential for both locals and tourists to rally behind conservation efforts. By educating both audiences about the importance of the natural world, conservation efforts can gain broader support.

The red-crowned crane park near the Sanjiang Plain in northeastern Heilongjiang Province is a prime example of how local communities can benefit from conservation-minded tourism. This site demonstrates that locals can move beyond merely regarding conservation and ecosystem aspects and recognize the commercial and political advantages of supporting and promoting environmental research.

Bridging the Gap Between Perspectives

It is crucial to bridge the gap between Western and local views on environmental conservation in China. By fostering mutual understanding and cooperation, both sides can work together to address the environmental challenges and develop sustainable solutions that benefit both nature and communities.

13

CHAPTER 13: CHINESE LITERATURE: CLASSICAL MASTERPI

Over five millennia have passed, and there are 5,000 stories to tell. China's literature features a wide range of narrations, thoughts, and feelings, capturing extraordinary values and wisdom. With a wealth of classics such as *The Book of Songs*, *Chu Ci*, and *Han Shan*, and modern masterpieces in the 20th and 21st centuries such as *The Wilderness Trilogy* and *Red News*, Chinese literature carries extraordinary values, full of life wisdom.

Classical Masterpieces

Most classic Chinese novels focus on plot as the main creative source. Some of the greatest works include:

- **Three Kingdoms**
- **Outlaws of the Marsh**
- **Romance of the Three Kingdoms**

- **The Plum in the Golden Vase**
- **Journey to the West**

These novels reflect the spirit of their respective times, blending storytelling with historical context and philosophical insights. For example:

- **Chu Ci**, one of the earliest literature anthologies, focuses on lyrical themes.
- **Sima Qian's Historical Records** delve into past stories, integrating a realistic vision with the application of mystery to form a distinct blend of dynamic and static elements—philosophy.

These masterpieces transcend their ages and remain relevant today.

Modern and Contemporary Works

Chinese literature today is characterized by its diversity and inclusivity. In recent years, renowned authors such as Wang Shuo, Chi Li, and Yan Lianke have persisted in breaking boundaries. They turn their gaze to introspection and humanism, focusing on depicting the human heart and the true human spirit.

Modern masterpieces in the 20th and 21st centuries include:

- *Astrology*
- *Nine Places, You*
- *Do Not Say, My Face, If You Love Me*

These works have been published worldwide, showcasing the rich variety of narrations, thoughts, and feelings in contemporary Chinese literature.

Supporting Emerging Authors

Countless talented midstream and new authors are adding their voices to contemporary literature. The number of Chinese literature and art journals is soaring, providing support and attention to more authors. This growing platform for literary expression ensures that new and diverse voices continue to enrich Chinese literature.

14

CHAPTER 14: CHINESE MARTIAL ARTS: HISTORY, STYLES,

If you've spent any time posting on social media or searching for online videos displaying martial art techniques, you know that there are many different martial art styles around the world. Surprisingly, not every culture has developed its own martial tradition. However, in China, you'll encounter pharmacies specializing in herbs to heal common martial arts injuries and schools teaching children the fundamentals of one of the 10 major martial art families. After watching a local martial art master demonstrate a technique, you may decide to undertake learning kung-fu as well.

The History of Chinese Martial Arts

The history of martial arts in China is as long and storied as the Great Wall itself. Traveling warrior-singers and specialized units of martial artists defended caravans of goods for hire, and over hundreds of years, martial arts played a significant role in shaping Chinese society.

In 1911, the "Xinhai Revolution" established the Republic of China, placing the world's first republic in the hands of its elected leader. In 1928, the country was re-unified for the first time in almost 3,000 years. In this new world order, every style of martial arts, along with a variety of internal and external kung-fu, was taught and developed.

Styles of Chinese Martial Arts

Chinese martial arts are incredibly diverse, with each style offering unique techniques and philosophies. Some of the most prominent styles include:

- **Shaolin Kung Fu**: Known for its strength and agility, this style is closely associated with the Shaolin Monastery and is famous for its rigorous training methods and powerful strikes.
- **Tai Chi**: A gentle, flowing martial art that emphasizes balance, flexibility, and inner peace. It is often practiced for its health benefits and meditative qualities.
- **Wing Chun**: A close-combat style that focuses on quick, efficient movements and direct strikes. It is designed to be practical and effective in real-world self-defense situations.
- **Wushu**: Modern Wushu retains the acrobatics and kicking skills of northern styles but incorporates elements of dance, adding difficult agility, twists, and high jumps.

Philosophy and Practice

Chinese martial arts are deeply rooted in philosophical principles, such as those found in Confucianism, Taoism, and Buddhism. These philosophies emphasize balance, harmony, and the cultivation of both physical and mental strength. Martial arts practice is seen as a way to achieve self-discipline, inner peace, and personal growth.

- **Qi (Chi)**: Central to many styles is the concept of Qi, the vital life force that flows through the body. Martial arts training aims to cultivate and control Qi to enhance physical abilities and overall well-being.
- **Self-Discipline and Respect**: Practitioners are taught to respect their teachers, fellow students, and the art itself. Self-discipline is key to mastering the techniques and philosophies of martial arts.

Modern Influence

Today, Chinese martial arts continue to evolve, blending traditional techniques with modern training methods. Schools and practitioners around the world are dedicated to preserving the rich heritage of Chinese martial arts while also adapting to contemporary needs and interests.

15

CHAPTER 15: RELIGIOUS DIVERSITY IN CHINA: DAOISM,

The Chinese are said to be pragmatic: Confucian in attitude and Daoist in practice. They believe in order, ancestors, and heaven but often do not strictly adhere to organized religion. Nevertheless, China's belief systems are diverse and all-encompassing. China is home to twenty-five percent of the world's religious practitioners, who practice Daoism (Taoism), Buddhism, Islam, and Christianity. The country is noted for its calm tolerance and spiritual equanimity, hosting a wide array of beliefs including Falun Gong and Protestantism among other denominations.

Daoism (Taoism)

Daoism, or Taoism, is a homegrown Chinese religion and philosophy that emphasizes living in harmony with the Tao (the Way), an underlying principle that is the source and force behind everything that exists. Daoist practices include meditation, feng shui, and the pursuit of longevity and immortality through various spiritual exercises.

Buddhism

Buddhism, an Eastern religion that originated in ancient India, has been instrumental in shaping China's pantheon of beliefs. Buddhism focuses on the path to enlightenment through practices such as meditation, ethical living, and the understanding of the Four Noble Truths. It has deeply influenced Chinese culture, arts, and philosophy.

Islam

Islam, the predominant religion in the western regions of China, has a significant following among the Hui, Uighur, Kazakh, and other ethnic groups. Chinese Muslims practice Islam while maintaining their distinct cultural identities. The religion promotes the worship of Allah and follows the teachings of the Prophet Muhammad.

Christianity

Christianity, comprising Roman Catholicism, Protestantism, and Orthodoxy, took time to establish in China. The Chinese empire once prided itself on its own divinity, with the emperor symbolizing the midpoint between heaven and earth. Christianity introduced a different sort of deity—Jesus, as the intercessor, and Muhammad in the context of Islam.

According to historical census statistics from the Palladius in its March 1905 issue, there were 197,606 Roman Catholics, 29,868 Protestant Christians, and over a million Orthodox in China. These three forms of Christianity constitute about 5% of Chinese religious belief today.

Religious Tolerance and Diversity

China's religious diversity reflects its long history of cultural exchange and philosophical openness. Despite challenges, the country continues to be a place where multiple religions coexist, and many Chinese people blend traditional practices with modern beliefs. This complex tapestry of faiths contributes to the rich spiritual and cultural landscape of China.

16

CHAPTER 16: WOMEN IN CHINESE SOCIETY: PAST AND PRE

Women have always played an important role in Chinese civilization, not just as wives and mothers, but also as poets, artists, and political figures. However, over the centuries, women of different classes, regions, and time periods have experienced dramatically different lives. This chapter will take readers behind the scenes to explore what it has meant—and still means—to be a woman in China. We will delve into historical and political contexts that have shaped the traditional and modern experiences of Chinese women.

Historical Roles of Women

Ancient Legends and Influential Figures

In ancient China, women like the legendary empress Nüwa, who is said to have fixed the problems of the world that the pantheon allowed to occur, played significant roles in myths and legends. Nüwa, for instance, is credited with creating humanity and repairing the sky, highlighting the revered position some female figures held in Chinese mythology.

Female Participation in Art and Literature

Throughout the great classical Chinese dynasties, women participated in art and literature, contributing to the cultural and intellectual life of their times. Women poets such as Li Qingzhao from the Song Dynasty and painters like Guan Daosheng from the Yuan Dynasty are notable examples of female talent and influence. These women defied the norms of their eras to make significant contributions to Chinese culture.

The Practice of Footbinding

One of the most physically and mentally rigorous practices that Chinese women endured was footbinding. This practice, which began in the Song Dynasty and lasted for almost a thousand years, involved tightly binding young girls' feet to alter their shape. Footbinding was seen as a symbol of beauty and status but caused lifelong pain and disability. The practice eventually ended in the early 20th century due to changing social norms and increased awareness of its detrimental effects.

Modern Roles of Women
Women in Contemporary China

In modern China, women's roles have evolved significantly. The founding of the People's Republic of China in 1949 marked a new era for women, with the government promoting gender equality and women's rights. Women today occupy prominent positions in politics, business, and academia, breaking barriers that once confined them to domestic roles.

Education and Employment

Education has been a critical area of progress for Chinese women. The emphasis on universal education has enabled women to pursue higher education and professional careers. The presence of women in universities and their participation in various fields, from science to the arts, showcases the strides made towards gender equality.

Rural and Urban Experiences

The experiences of women in rural and urban China can differ significantly. Rural women often face challenges related to traditional gender roles and limited access to education and healthcare. However, many have become entrepreneurs and community leaders, contributing to the rural economy. In contrast, urban women may have greater access to education and career opportunities but also face the pressures of balancing work and family life.

Case Studies

Village Woman Taking University Entrance Exams

Consider the case of a village woman preparing for the university entrance exams. Her journey is marked by determination and resilience as she balances household responsibilities with her studies. Her success can inspire other young women in rural areas to pursue education and strive for better opportunities.

Empress in Qing Dynasty China

In Qing Dynasty China, empresses wielded significant influence within the imperial court. Empress Dowager Cixi, for instance, played a crucial role in the political affairs of the Qing Dynasty. Her life, marked by power struggles and political maneuvers, highlights the complex roles women could play in Chinese history.

Women's History and Literature

Contributions to Literature

The literary contributions of Chinese women are vast and varied. From classical poetry to contemporary novels, female authors have used their writings to express their thoughts, emotions, and social critiques. Authors like Eileen Chang and contemporary writers such as Xiaolu Guo have gained international recognition for their work.

Women's Rights Movements

The women's rights movements in China have been instrumental in advancing gender equality. Activists have campaigned for legal reforms, better working conditions, and social recognition of women's contributions. The efforts of these movements continue to shape the discourse on gender equality in China today.

17

CHAPTER 17: EDUCATION SYSTEM IN CHINA: HISTORICAL

Historically, China has always been renowned for the wisdom of its people. The emphasis of the early educational tradition was on the importance of scholarship. To develop training and ensure high qualifications for students, a system of national examinations was introduced. Education provided people with numerous opportunities for intellectual and moral pursuits.

Historical Development

Confucian Beginnings

The roots of Chinese education can be traced back to the teachings of the philosopher and thinker Confucius (551-479 BC). Confucianism emphasized the importance of education, moral development, and civic responsibility. This early tradition laid the groundwork for a culture that values learning and intellectual achievement.

National Examinations

To ensure the quality and qualification of scholars, a system of national examinations was established. This meritocratic system allowed individuals from various backgrounds to rise to prominent positions based on their intellectual capabilities. The Imperial Examination System, which began during the Sui Dynasty (581-618 AD), became a cornerstone of Chinese education for over a thousand years.

Twentieth Century Reforms

During the twentieth century, the Chinese government underwent at least four significant periods of educational reform. These reforms aimed to modernize the education system and adapt it to the changing needs of society.

Early Twentieth Century Reforms

In the early 1900s, China began to reform its education system to incorporate Western educational models. These reforms focused on modernizing curriculum and pedagogy, introducing subjects like science and mathematics, and emphasizing practical skills.

Post-1949 Reforms

The establishment of the People's Republic of China in 1949 marked a significant turning point in Chinese education. A national educational system uniformly regulated by the state was introduced. This period saw the creation of kindergarten institutions and education for handicapped people. Elementary schools were extended, and many new institutions of higher learning were established.

Cultural Revolution Impact

The Cultural Revolution (1966-1976) had a profound impact on Chinese education. Schools were closed, and academic pursuits were devalued in favor of political indoctrination. Many educators and intellectuals were persecuted, and the education system suffered significant setbacks.

Reform and Opening-Up Era

The late 1970s and 1980s marked the beginning of the Reform and Opening-Up era, which revitalized the education system. Emphasis was placed on economic development and modernization, leading to the expansion of higher education and the promotion of scientific and technological research.

Modern Reforms and Development

The modern Chinese education system builds on years of experience and practice from early educational traditions and modern approaches to education. The system is developing successfully, with a steadily growing number of students and educational institutions. Chinese education today is open to improvement and opportunities for international collaboration.

Expansion of Higher Education

The number of universities and tertiary institutions has increased significantly. Higher education is now accessible to a broader population, including foreign students. Tertiary education institutions offer a wide range of programs, from technical schools to professional degrees and universities.

Emphasis on Quality and Innovation

Modern reforms focus on improving the quality of education, incorporating innovative teaching methods, and integrating technology into the classroom. The Chinese government is committed to making education more inclusive and equitable, ensuring that all students have access to quality education.

Internationalization of Education

Chinese education is increasingly international, with many students studying abroad and foreign students coming to China. Collaborative programs and partnerships with international institutions enhance the global perspective of Chinese education.

Challenges and Future Directions

Despite significant progress, the Chinese education system faces challenges such as regional disparities, pressure on students due to intense competition, and the need for continuous improvement in teaching quality. The future direction of Chinese education will likely focus on addressing these challenges, fostering innovation, and further integrating global educational standards.

18

CHAPTER 18: CHINESE FILM INDUSTRY: FROM CLASSICS T

The value of an artistic output is often thought of in terms of its universality, but its reception and interpretation can undergo profound changes in different localities. While Hong Kong's charts might show impressive box-office hits, Taiwan's theatergoers often prefer a completely different array of genres and stars. As diverse as the Mandarin-speaking communities are, so are their media production spaces and intensities.

Diverse Media Landscapes

The film studios of mainland China produce classics and blockbusters, similar to every other major film industry worldwide. Light-hearted comedies from southern Taiwan make regular cross-strait profits, though sometimes grudgingly on the Taiwanese people's part. Meanwhile, folk and city dwellers from Beijing's backyard consume the same budget comedies of southern-

Beijing collaborations, enjoying a completely different ring in terms of dialect from the Taiwanese ones.

This diversity illustrates the point that beneath the popularity and profitability of audio-visual creations lie stark differences in geopolitical tastes and sociocultural nature. Despite marketers' efforts to portray their products as fitting every pocket and all seasons, various conditions—linguistic, tax code adherence, culture, politics, and state of war—determine how far a 'second-order' film can travel and speak the tongue of the native.

Historical Context and Evolution

The Chinese film industry has a rich history, dating back to the early 20th century. It has gone through various phases, including the influence of political movements, the establishment of major film studios, and the introduction of new technologies. The industry has produced numerous classics that have left a lasting impact on both Chinese and global cinema.

- **Early Beginnings**: The first Chinese film, *Dingjun Mountain*, was made in 1905. The industry saw rapid growth in the 1920s and 1930s, producing silent films and early sound films that reflected Chinese society and culture.
- **Maoist Era**: During the 1950s and 1960s, the film industry became an important tool for political propaganda. Films produced during this period often depicted revolutionary themes and promoted socialist values.
- **Post-Cultural Revolution**: After the Cultural Revolution, the Chinese film industry began to di-

versify, producing films that explored a wider range of themes and narratives. The 1980s and 1990s saw the emergence of the "Fifth Generation" filmmakers, who gained international acclaim for their innovative storytelling and cinematography.

Modern Blockbusters and Global Influence

Today, the Chinese film industry is a powerhouse, producing blockbuster films that compete with Hollywood productions. Modern Chinese cinema is characterized by high production values, advanced special effects, and engaging storylines. Some of the most successful films have broken box-office records and gained international recognition.

- **Big-Budget Films**: Movies like *Wolf Warrior 2* and *The Wandering Earth* have set new standards for Chinese blockbusters, showcasing the industry's ability to produce action-packed and visually stunning films.
- **International Collaborations**: Chinese filmmakers increasingly collaborate with international studios, actors, and directors. These collaborations enhance the global appeal of Chinese films and promote cultural exchange.
- **Diverse Genres**: From historical dramas and martial arts epics to science fiction and romantic comedies, the Chinese film industry produces a wide range of genres that cater to diverse audiences.

Challenges and Opportunities

While the Chinese film industry has achieved significant success, it also faces challenges. These include navigating censorship regulations, balancing commercial success with artistic integrity, and addressing competition from international films. However, the industry's continued growth and innovation present numerous opportunities for filmmakers and audiences alike.

19

CHAPTER 19: SPACE EXPLORATION AND SCIENTIFIC ACHIE

Space programs are some of the most awe-inspiring endeavors carried out by humanity. Several nations have made great progress in their space exploration missions, and China has been no different. The country has become a pioneer in space exploration, demonstrating its capability to lead and shape the future of space technology.

Early Achievements

China's journey in space exploration began with the launch of its first satellite, **Dong Fang Hong 1**, in 1970, making it the fifth country ever to launch a satellite into space using its own methods. This milestone marked the beginning of China's ambitious space endeavors.

Lunar Exploration and Mars Missions

Since then, China has continued to chart new frontiers through its ambitious plans to explore the Moon and Mars. The country has built its first lunar sample return spacecraft, **Chang'e 6**, based on the spacecraft models of the **Chang'e 7** mission. These missions are part of China's larger lunar exploration program aimed at understanding the Moon's composition and geology.

Mars Ambitions

China's Mars exploration program includes plans to colonize Mars and conduct in-depth studies of the planet. The country is also collaborating with the Russian space agency on a program to return samples of Martian soil to Earth. This collaboration signifies China's commitment to international partnerships in advancing space science.

Quantum Computing and Scientific Advancements

Chinese scientists have made significant progress in developing time-dependent variables in superconducting qubits. Led by researchers such as Wang, Tuo Tan, Dao Zhang, Yipu Song, and Dongning Zheng, the **Integrated Quantum Computing Project** at the University of Science and Technology of China (USTC) has investigated the time dependence of fluctuations and decoherence in superconducting quantum bits.

Quantum Points and Environmental Variables

Research advances in using quantum points to quantify important environmental variables and in accurately measuring high-precision static magnetic fields have contributed to the growing use of artificial quantum states in the field of quantum information processing. These developments highlight China's capabilities in cutting-edge scientific research and technological innovation.

Future Prospects

China's ambitious space exploration plans include exploring near-Earth asteroids and furthering its Mars missions. The nation's investments in space technology and scientific research underscore its determination to be a leading force in the global space community.

20

CHAPTER 20: BELT AND ROAD INITIATIVE: CONNECTING C

This chapter presents a detailed overview of China's cultural, socioeconomic, and historic heritage as a synthesis of ancient traditions and values alongside rapid modernization and innovation. Covering 20 key themes and an array of subtopics ranging from scenic and natural sites to cuisine and regional specialties, legendary and historical figures, and traditional artistic, architectural, and religious traditions, it discusses the diversity, complexity, and depth of these topics. Each subtopic provides points for discussion or consideration for tourists, underlining the informational value for those preparing to visit China.

The Belt and Road Initiative (BRI)

The Belt and Road Initiative (BRI) is one of the most extensive and ambitious economic projects in modern history. It comprises land and sea economic logistics and communication corridors, underpinned by a 'common development' political framework. As part of the BRI, China is working to build economic and political partnerships with, and foster friendship and mutual respect among, individuals, political leaders, private businesspeople, religious and social organizations, and children across predominantly Eurasia. The goal is to create 'shared common weal for all citizens' in an environment of trade investment aimed at a broader social and political outlook that treats the greater good as a starting point, as opposed to prioritizing the interests of a few wealthy Western countries.

Land and Sea Corridors

The BRI includes two main components:

- **The Silk Road Economic Belt**: This land-based component aims to connect China with Central Asia, Europe, and the Middle East through a network of railways, highways, and pipelines.
- **The 21st Century Maritime Silk Road**: This sea-based component seeks to link China with Southeast Asia, South Asia, Africa, and Europe via major sea routes.

Objectives and Goals

The primary objectives of the BRI are:

- **Economic Integration**: Promote economic cooperation and integration among participating countries.

- **Infrastructure Development**: Enhance infrastructure connectivity to facilitate trade and investment.
- **Cultural Exchange**: Foster cultural exchange and mutual understanding between diverse cultures.
- **Sustainable Development**: Encourage sustainable development practices and environmentally friendly projects.

Key Projects

Several key projects under the BRI include:

- **China–Pakistan Economic Corridor (CPEC)**: A collection of infrastructure projects aimed at improving connectivity between China and Pakistan.
- **New Eurasian Land Bridge**: A rail link connecting China to Europe, facilitating faster and more efficient trade routes.
- **Port Development**: Expansion and modernization of ports in countries such as Sri Lanka, Greece, and Djibouti to enhance maritime trade routes.

Global Implications and Challenges

The BRI has far-reaching implications for global trade, economics, and geopolitics. It aims to reshape global trade routes and foster closer ties between participating countries. However, the initiative also faces challenges, including:

- **Debt Concerns**: Participating countries' potential debt burden due to large-scale infrastructure projects.
- **Geopolitical Tensions**: Strategic concerns and competition with other global powers.
- **Environmental Impact**: Ensuring that development projects are sustainable and environmentally friendly.

Conclusion

The Belt and Road Initiative is a testament to China's vision of global connectivity and cooperation. It represents an important layer of context for tourists and scholars alike to consider, engage with, and debate. The BRI's success will depend on the collaboration and mutual respect of all participating nations, aiming to create a more interconnected and prosperous world.

21

CHAPTER 21: TRADITIONAL CHINESE ARCHITECTURE: TEMP

When considering the architectural heritage of China, people often first imagine temples, pagodas, and gardens. These architectural wonders offer a glimpse into the mindset of ancient China and the artists who designed these spaces as reflections of universal principles. Some of the oldest standing wooden structures in the world, including pagodas in China, are multi-eaved towers of worship for both Buddhists and Daoists.

Temples

Temples in China are not only religious centers but also masterpieces of traditional architecture. They often feature intricate carvings, statues of deities, and beautifully painted murals. These sacred spaces are designed to foster spiritual contemplation and worship.

- **Buddhist Temples**: One of the most famous examples is the Shaolin Temple, known for its association with martial arts and Buddhism. The Longmen Grottoes are another example, with thousands of Buddha statues carved into cliffs.
- **Daoist Temples**: Daoist temples, such as the White Cloud Temple in Beijing, are characterized by their serene environments and harmonious designs, reflecting Daoist principles of nature and balance.

Pagodas

Pagodas are iconic structures in Chinese architecture, often built to house religious relics. They symbolize the connection between heaven and earth and are used for worship and meditation. These multi-tiered towers come in various shapes and sizes, each with its unique style.

- **Wooden Pagodas**: The Wooden Pagoda of Yingxian, built during the Liao Dynasty, is the tallest wooden pagoda in the world and a prime example of ancient Chinese engineering.
- **Brick Pagodas**: The Giant Wild Goose Pagoda in Xi'an, constructed during the Tang Dynasty, is a brick pagoda that has stood the test of time, symbolizing cultural and spiritual continuity.

Gardens

Chinese gardens are designed to emulate natural landscapes in a condensed form. They reflect the harmony found in nature and provide a space for reflection and tranquility. The design of these gardens incorporates various elements such as water, rocks, plants, and architecture to create a balanced and aesthetically pleasing environment.

- **Classical Gardens of Suzhou**: Known for their meticulous design and natural beauty, these gardens include famous sites like the Humble Administrator's Garden and the Lingering Garden. They are UNESCO World Heritage Sites and exemplify traditional Chinese garden design.
- **Imperial Gardens**: The Summer Palace in Beijing is a sprawling complex of lakes, gardens, and palaces that served as a retreat for the imperial family. Its design reflects the natural beauty and harmony that traditional Chinese gardens strive to achieve.

Architectural Philosophy

The philosophy behind traditional Chinese architecture is deeply rooted in nature and the principles of harmony and balance. Whether it's a temple, pagoda, or garden, the design aims to create a space where humans can live in harmony with their surroundings and find peace and inspiration.

- **Nature and Harmony**: Traditional Chinese architecture incorporates elements of nature, presenting them in a way that emphasizes their inherent beauty and harmony. This approach is intended to inspire reflection and spiritual growth.

· **Art and Function**: These structures are not only functional but also serve as works of art. The intricate designs, detailed carvings, and thoughtful layouts reflect the artistic and cultural values of ancient China.

22

CHAPTER 22: CHINESE MUSIC: FROM TRADITIONAL INSTRU

When we think about the ancient heritage and modern wonders of China, one of the first things that might come to mind is Chinese music. Indeed, the musical legacy of this country is both ancient and vast, and the traditions continue to be richly celebrated in China and around the world. Let's explore the sounds of China, ranging from traditional Chinese music instruments to the latest in Chinese singers and groups.

Traditional Chinese Music

Ancient Instruments

Traditional Chinese music is deeply rooted in the country's history and culture. Some of the oldest musical instruments include:

- **Guqin**: The Chinese zither, a seven-stringed instrument, has been played for over 3,000 years and is associated with scholars and sages.
- **Bamboo Flute**: Known as the **dizi**, this instrument produces a clear, melodious sound and is one of the oldest Chinese instruments.

In addition to these, there are many other traditional and unique Chinese musical instruments:

- **Erhu**: A two-string fiddle played with a bow, producing a soulful and expressive sound.
- **Pipa**: A plucked lute with a fretted fingerboard, known for its delicate and intricate melodies.
- **Sheng**: A mouth organ with multiple pipes, creating a rich and harmonious sound.
- **Yangqin**: A hammered dulcimer, producing a bright and percussive tone.
- **Dizi**: A flute or panpipes, known for its versatile and vibrant sound.

Classical and Folk Music

Chinese classical and folk music orchestras feature these instruments in various ensembles:

- **Beijing Opera and Kunqu Opera**: These traditional Chinese opera forms incorporate classical instruments to create dramatic and emotional performances.
- **Yunnan Southern Dancers' Pipe Orchestra**: Known for its folksy sound, this orchestra uses

traditional instruments to perform lively and spirited music.

- **Hmong Ancestor Worship Ceremony in SW Guizhou**: The pentatonic scales used in these ceremonies create a unique and haunting musical experience.

Modern Chinese Music
Contemporary Artists and Pop Music

The Chinese music scene has evolved to include a diverse range of genres, from traditional to modern pop. Contemporary Chinese artists and pop groups have gained immense popularity both domestically and internationally.

- **Jay Chou**: Known as the "King of Mandopop," Jay Chou has revolutionized the Chinese pop music scene with his innovative blend of pop, rock, and classical elements.
- **Faye Wong**: A legendary singer and actress, Faye Wong is renowned for her ethereal voice and contributions to C-pop and alternative music.
- **TFBoys**: A popular boy band that has captured the hearts of millions of fans, combining catchy tunes with impressive dance routines.
- **G.E.M.**: A versatile singer-songwriter who has achieved fame for her powerful vocals and heartfelt lyrics.

Fusion and Innovation

Modern Chinese music often incorporates traditional elements, creating a fusion of old and new:

- **Electronic Music**: Artists like Zhang Yadong and Lay Zhang have experimented with electronic beats, blending them with traditional Chinese instruments.
- **Rock and Indie Music**: Bands like "Carsick Cars" and "New Pants" have brought a fresh perspective to the Chinese music scene, infusing rock and indie styles with local influences.

Conclusion

Chinese music, from its ancient roots to modern innovations, offers a rich tapestry of sounds and styles. Traditional instruments and classical performances continue to be celebrated, while contemporary artists push the boundaries of creativity and genre. This dynamic blend of old and new makes Chinese music a vibrant and ever-evolving cultural force.

23

CHAPTER 23: SOCIAL MEDIA AND TECHNOLOGY TRENDS IN

Today, Chinese people prefer navigating, making friends, dating, booking restaurants and tickets, and entertainment through social media above any other methods. As of now, WeChat and Weibo each have over 560 million active users—numbers we can barely even imagine in the United States. WeChat has become an all-in-one lifestyle app where you can link up bank accounts, manage your planning and shopping, send messages and make group chats, and navigate travel maps while sharing your stories. In short, without getting involved in China's social media presence, full awareness of any trend is simply incomplete.

Social Media Giants

WeChat

WeChat, known as Weixin in China, is not just a messaging app but a comprehensive platform that integrates multiple functions. Users can:

- **Connect**: Link bank accounts, manage finances, and make payments.
- **Organize**: Schedule plans, book tickets, and navigate using maps.
- **Communicate**: Send messages, make group chats, and share stories.
- **Engage**: Follow official accounts, participate in mini-programs, and access various services.

WeChat has transformed how people interact with technology, making everyday tasks more convenient and efficient.

Weibo

Weibo, often compared to Twitter, is a microblogging platform that allows users to post updates, share content, and engage with followers. It serves as a vital tool for:

- **News**: Real-time updates and trending topics.
- **Entertainment**: Interactions with celebrities and influencers.
- **Marketing**: Brands use Weibo for promotions and customer engagement.

Technological Advancements

China prides itself on having advanced technology and web systems, which have made it easy to "smarten" up and launch various smart technologies: smart homes, cars, cities, airports, and industries. China's technological development is showcased during live broadcasts, e-commerce scenarios, and TV programs, renewing various physical outlets with a range of tech features on a daily basis.

Smart Technologies

Smart Homes: Integrated systems that control lighting, temperature, security, and appliances remotely.

- **Smart Cities**: Infrastructure that uses data and technology to improve urban living, transportation, and resource management.
- **Smart Airports**: Enhanced travel experiences with automated check-ins, facial recognition, and efficient baggage handling.
- **Smart Industries**: Factories and production lines that utilize robotics, AI, and IoT for increased productivity and efficiency.

Cool Live Demonstrations

Chinese company employees leverage the country's tech-leading position to conduct impressive live demonstrations:

- **Robot Dogs**: Guiding visitors and providing assistance.
- **Facial Recognition Check-In**: Validating orders with a simple wave in cashier-less stores.
- **Multi-Layer Luggage Reclaim Robots**: Scanning QR codes to receive baggage conveniently.

These technologies exemplify China's commitment to innovation and the practical applications of cutting-edge advancements.

Impact on Traditional Marketing

Social media's impact is rapidly transforming traditional marketing, transcending national boundaries. Brands and businesses utilize social media platforms to reach broader audiences, engage with customers, and create personalized marketing campaigns. The integration of social media in marketing strategies is essential for staying relevant in the competitive market.

24

CHAPTER 24: ONE COUNTRY, TWO SYSTEMS: HONG KONG AN

The principle of "One Country, Two Systems" embodies a unique constitutional and governance framework established to integrate Hong Kong and Macau into China while preserving their distinct political, legal, and economic systems for 50 years following their sovereignty reversion. This arrangement was agreed upon by the Chinese government and the respective colonial powers—Britain for Hong Kong and Portugal for Macau—prior to the handover in 1997 and 1999, respectively. The framework is enshrined in the Basic Laws of the Hong Kong and Macau Special Administrative Regions (SARs), which function as mini-constitutions for these territories.

Under this arrangement, Hong Kong and Macau maintain significant autonomy in various domains, including their legal systems, monetary policies, and immigration controls. These territories operate under the governance structures and legal traditions of their colonial predecessors—British common law for Hong Kong and Portuguese civil law for Macau. The Chinese government, through the National People's Congress (NPC), oversees and ensures the implementation of the "One Country, Two Systems" policy, with the NPC passing laws to define the principles of this governance model.

Governance and Elections

The Basic Law of Hong Kong, adopted in 1990, outlines a gradual progression toward greater democratization, with the ultimate goal being the election of the Chief Executive by universal suffrage. Currently, the Chief Executive is selected by an Election Committee, a body composed of representatives from various sectors of society. While this structure was intended as a transitional measure, it has been a source of controversy. Critics argue that the process limits genuine democratic participation, as the Election Committee is often perceived to reflect the interests of Beijing.

Article 45 of the Hong Kong Basic Law sets universal suffrage as a long-term goal, yet its implementation has faced delays and political challenges. Similar challenges exist in Macau, where plans for the direct election of the Chief Executive by universal suffrage remain unrealized. The governance structure in Macau mirrors that of Hong Kong, with the Chief Executive selected by an Election Committee.

Legal Autonomy and Judicial Independence

A cornerstone of the "One Country, Two Systems" framework is the preservation of legal autonomy and judicial independence in Hong Kong and Macau. The Basic Laws guarantee freedoms such as free speech, press freedom, and judicial independence, aligning with international standards. In Hong Kong, British common law traditions remain in force, while Macau continues to apply Portuguese civil law as it stood on December 19, 1999.

However, this legal autonomy is not absolute. The Chinese Constitution allows the central government to intervene under specific circumstances, such as issues concerning national security, public order, and health. In Macau, for instance, Beijing retains the authority to amend or override local laws if they conflict with national interests or legislative frameworks established by the central government.

Challenges and Controversies

Despite the guarantees of autonomy, the implementation of "One Country, Two Systems" has faced significant challenges. In Hong Kong, tensions have arisen over perceived encroachments by Beijing on the city's freedoms and autonomy, leading to widespread protests, particularly concerning electoral reforms and national security laws.

In Macau, the transition has been less contentious, partly due to its smaller population and traditionally less politically active civil society. Nonetheless, concerns persist regarding the long-term preservation of autonomy, especially as the 50-year mark approaches in 2047 for Hong Kong and 2049 for Macau.

Conclusion

"One Country, Two Systems" represents a bold and unprecedented experiment in governance, balancing the sovereignty of a single nation with the autonomy of two distinct regions. While the framework has provided a degree of stability and continuity, its long-term success will depend on addressing political tensions, ensuring genuine democratic progress, and maintaining the rule of law and freedoms promised in the Basic Laws. The evolution of this arrangement continues to draw global attention, serving as a test case for managing complex sovereignty and autonomy relationships.

25

CHAPTER 25: TIBET AND XINJIANG: ETHNIC MINORITIES

Tibet: A Land of Rich Culture and Natural Beauty

Tibet, often referred to as the "Land of the Snows," is a region with a rich tapestry of culture and history. The strong observance of Buddhism in Tibet has led to cultural similarities with other Buddhist regions such as Bhutan, Mongolia, and Nepal. Despite its underdeveloped industries and weak infrastructure, Tibet offers stunning landscapes and pristine lakes that attract intrepid tourists. Visitors can enjoy hot springs, beautiful resorts in the Tibetan capital of Lhasa, and cultural celebrations such as the annual Great Prayer held in the Drepung Monastery and Samye Monastery.

Xinjiang: A Region of Unique Muslim Culture

To the northwest of China lies Xinjiang, a region predominantly home to the Uighur people. The Muslim

91

culture in Xinjiang is unique due to the centuries-old connections to Persia. Although there are few remaining traces of Persian settlements, the influence of Persian culture is still evident. In recent years, the Chinese government has implemented sweeping plans to assimilate minority people in Xinjiang into the Han Chinese majority. Gülbahar Jelilova, a Uighur activist, has reported that millions of Muslims are detained in political re-education facilities in Xinjiang. The Chinese government has allocated an estimated US$1 billion to construct these facilities, which primarily target minority Uighurs and Kazakhs.

Surveillance and Repression in Xinjiang

The Chinese government's anti-Muslim policies and crackdown on the Uighur people have led to unprecedented levels of surveillance in Xinjiang. The government has placed a travel ban on Tibet, motivated by fears of political instability. Statistics show that Tibetan ownership of tourism and traditional Chinese economy is vastly excluded, prompting Tibetan habilitation and migration to coastal eastern regions. As a nation with many ethnic minorities, China's policies of assimilation foster social equity through conformity rather than cultural preservation.

Conclusion

China's policies towards ethnic minorities in Tibet and Xinjiang highlight the challenges of cultural preservation in the face of assimilation efforts. While Tibet offers a rich cultural heritage and natural beauty, Xinjiang's unique Muslim culture faces significant repression and surveillance. Understanding these regions' dynamics is crucial for grasping the broader context of China's approach to ethnic minorities and cultural preservation.

26

CHAPTER 26: TERRACOTTA ARMY: DISCOVERY, SIGNIFICAN

Discovery of the Terracotta Army

The Terracotta Army, also known as the "Terracotta Warriors and Horses," was discovered by accident in 1974 by a group of Chinese farmers digging a well. This incredible archaeological find is presumed to have been created to accompany the first Emperor of China, Qin Shi Huang (Qin Shi Huangdi), into the afterlife. The military aspect of the site likely served as a protective force for the emperor in the afterlife. Since their discovery, the Terracotta Warriors have intrigued historians, archaeologists, and the general population, becoming one of the most remarkable and important historical sites in the world.

Significance of the Terracotta Army

The Terracotta Army is significant for several reasons:

- **Historical Insight**: The site provides valuable insights into the military, cultural, and technological aspects of ancient China. Each warrior is unique, with distinct facial features, uniforms, and weapons, reflecting the diversity and complexity of the Qin Dynasty's army.
- **Scale and Scope**: The sheer number of soldiers, horses, and chariots involved—estimated to be around 8,000 soldiers, 130 chariots with 520 horses, and 150 cavalry horses—makes the Terracotta Army a monumental achievement in ancient craftsmanship and organization.
- **Cultural Heritage**: The Terracotta Army is a UNESCO World Heritage Site and a symbol of China's rich cultural heritage. It attracts millions of visitors each year, contributing to both local and national tourism.

Preservation Efforts

Preserving the Terracotta Army presents significant challenges due to the delicate nature of the artifacts. During the initial excavations and restoration, the colors of the warriors faded quickly as the lacquer began to harden, and cracks formed on their surfaces. To address these issues, various preservation techniques have been developed and implemented:

- **Maintaining Moisture**: The lacquer and paint on the warriors are extremely delicate and must stay moist to be preserved properly. Special measures are taken to control the humidity and temperature at the site to prevent further deterioration.
- **Innovative Techniques**: Recent advances in preservation technology show promise in retaining the lacquer and paint on the 2,000-year-old relics. These new methods involve the use of modern materials and techniques to stabilize and protect the ancient artifacts.
- **Comprehensive Conservation Plans**: Archaeological and engineering researchers have initiated comprehensive conservation plans to ensure the long-term preservation of the Terracotta Army. These efforts include developing new preservation methods and improving the living conditions for the tens of thousands of farmers living near the site.

Future Prospects

The future of the Terracotta Army's preservation looks promising, with ongoing research and technological advancements paving the way for more effective conservation methods. The combination of innovative techniques and comprehensive conservation plans will help protect this invaluable cultural heritage for future generations to appreciate.

27

CHAPTER 27: WILDLIFE CONSERVATION AND ENDANGERED S

Efforts in Wildlife Conservation
China is currently at the forefront of international efforts to save the environment, and this includes the preservation of the plants and animals that naturally live there. The central idea behind all of the wildlife conservation efforts in China is the desire to pass on as much of the natural world as possible to future generations. China is one of the last strongholds for several dozen types of rare and endangered birds and more than 160 types of rare and endangered mammals.

Endangered Species and Protection Efforts
Endemic Species
According to the catalog of the International Union for Conservation of Nature (IUCN), there are 32 types of animals living in China, 13 of them being endemic, which are categorized and protected in the appendix of

the Convention of Biological Diversity in China. Approximately 144 types of animals are listed by the World Wide Fund for Nature (WWF) and are protected similarly.

China boasts the largest number of wild mammals and birds in the world, with a total of 417 types of birds and 286 species of wild mammals. Additionally, the country is home to more than 30,000 plant species.

Conservation Challenges

However, the rapid economic development in China has brought about many environmental problems. The demand for timber, petrochemicals, and aquatic and marine products has been dominant globally since the reform era. This economic growth has led to several challenges in wildlife conservation:

- **Illegal Trade and Poaching**: The illegal trade of wildlife and poaching are significant threats to many species in China. These activities often target endangered animals, leading to further population declines.
- **Habitat Loss**: Urbanization, industrialization, and agricultural expansion contribute to the loss of natural habitats, which are crucial for the survival of many species.
- **Pollution**: Industrial pollution and the use of pesticides and herbicides in agriculture negatively impact wildlife and their habitats.

Conservation Initiatives and Programs

To address these challenges, China has implemented various conservation initiatives and programs aimed at protecting endangered species and preserving natural habitats:

- **Protected Areas**: Establishing nature reserves and national parks to provide safe habitats for endangered species and promote biodiversity conservation.
- **Anti-Poaching Measures**: Strengthening law enforcement to combat illegal trade and poaching, along with public awareness campaigns to reduce demand for wildlife products.
- **Reforestation Projects**: Initiating reforestation and afforestation programs to restore degraded habitats and increase forest cover.
- **Sustainable Development**: Promoting sustainable practices in agriculture, forestry, and fisheries to minimize environmental impact and ensure the long-term health of ecosystems.

Conclusion

China's efforts in wildlife conservation highlight the importance of preserving biodiversity for future generations. Despite facing significant challenges due to rapid economic development, the country is committed to protecting its unique flora and fauna. Continued investment in conservation initiatives and sustainable development practices will be crucial in ensuring the survival of endangered species in China.

28

CHAPTER 28: CHINESE FASHION AND TEXTILE INDUSTRY

Historical Roots of Chinese Textiles

The Chinese fashion and textile industry has a rich and storied history, with its roots tracing back to ancient China. Over time, the manufacture of silk became the cornerstone of Chinese textile artifacts. By the III-II centuries BC, the Chinese Empire earned global fame as the "Silk Empire," with all its silk being highly prized and sought after.

Imperial China is often associated with its distinctive fabrics featuring dragon motifs. Dragons were highly revered, symbolizing power and imperial authority. Artistic products without dragons were seldom presented to the Celestial Throne. An example of this reverence is the Pope's precious collection, which includes a special kimono made of brocade fabric embroidered with a golden dragon, signifying divine imperial power.

The Song Dynasty and Fashion Excellence

At the end of the 10th and the beginning of the 13th century, the disintegration of the Tang Empire led to the formation of six Chinese states, which eventually united into the Song Dynasty. During this period, the Chinese faced Europeans on a basis of "equality," though this concept of equality was not even recognized by the so-called "Diaoyu islanders."

The clothing culture during the Song Dynasty reached unparalleled levels of sophistication. The refined elegance of Chinese clothing was so esteemed that the daughter of the Song Emperor, clad in her most exquisite garments, attended official banquets only in the closest vestments—a testament to the meticulous attention to detail in Chinese fashion.

Modern Chinese Textile Industry

Fast forward to modern times, China has become a global leader in textile production. The country is known for manufacturing a significant portion of the world's clothing. The modern textile industry in China continues to build on its historical legacy, integrating traditional techniques with contemporary innovations.

Fashion and Celebrity Brands

Chinese fashion today is a blend of ancient traditions and modern trends. Celebrity brands and designers often draw inspiration from historical motifs and patterns, creating a unique fusion that appeals to both domestic and international markets. The enthusiasm for textile fashion and clothing in modern China is reflected in the works of contemporary designers who celebrate the rich heritage of Chinese textiles.

Challenges and Innovations

Despite its success, the Chinese textile industry faces several challenges, including environmental concerns, labor issues, and the need for sustainable practices. However, the industry is also at the forefront of innovation, with advancements in textile technology, eco-friendly materials, and efficient production methods.

Conclusion

The Chinese fashion and textile industry is a testament to the country's rich cultural heritage and its ability to adapt and innovate over time. From the ancient "Silk Empire" to modern-day fashion powerhouses, China's textile industry continues to be a key player in the global market, blending tradition with modernity to create timeless and stylish garments.

29

CHAPTER 29: SPORTS AND ATHLETICS IN CHINA: FROM PI

Historical Background
Some ancient texts in China mention athletic contests held among the various warring states in the run-up to unification by the state of Qin. However, during the Qing Dynasty, sports were poorly organized and nearly forgotten due to a focus on military and statecraft. Despite this, people still engaged in activities resembling sports. Community festivals and religious observances often featured various feats of strength, skills, and luck. For centuries, wrestling and martial arts have been regular parts of festivals and temple fairs across China.

The Rise of Modern Sports
The Chinese have also engaged in athletics as part of the process of coming together as a modern nation-state. One of the most well-known examples of this is

Ping-Pong diplomacy, which helped to thaw relations between Maoist China and the United States in the early 1970s.

China is one of the oldest homes of sports and physical culture. Dating back to the 4th century, the country is home to some of mankind's first sporting events, incorporating archery, wrestling, and chariot racing. While many of these ancient customs and games may no longer be practiced or relevant today, the modern Chinese have shown their adept skillsets in modern competitions and games.

Ping Pong (Table Tennis)

One of China's most notable contributions to modern sports is its dominance in table tennis, or ping pong. This sport has become synonymous with China's athletic prowess. The success of Chinese athletes in table tennis is evident in their impressive medal tally:

- **Olympic Success**: The Chinese ping pong team has taken home over 151 of the 249 gold medals presented since its inclusion in the 1988 Games in Seoul.
- **Global Competitions**: Chinese players consistently dominate international table tennis tournaments, showcasing their exceptional skills and dedication to the sport.

Olympic Achievements

China's participation in the Olympics has been marked by significant success across various sports:

- **Beijing 2008**: Hosting the Olympic Games in 2008 was a landmark moment for China. The country topped the medal table with 48 gold medals, showcasing its athletes' prowess across disciplines.
- **Tokyo 2020**: Competing in the recently concluded Tokyo Olympics, Chinese athletes continued to excel, adding numerous medals to the nation's tally.

Traditional and Modern Sports

Apart from table tennis, Chinese athletes have excelled in various traditional and modern sports:

- **Martial Arts**: Activities like wushu and kung fu have long been practiced in China, blending athleticism with cultural heritage.
- **Swimming**: China has produced world-class swimmers who have won numerous medals in international competitions.
- **Athletics**: Track and field events see strong representation from Chinese athletes, who have set records and won medals on the global stage.

Conclusion

From ancient athletic contests to modern Olympic success, sports and athletics in China have a rich and dynamic history. The country's achievements in table tennis, martial arts, and other sports highlight its commitment to excellence and its significant contributions to the global sports community.

30

CHAPTER 30: GREEN ENERGY AND SUSTAINABLE DEVELOPME

Green Energy: A National Strategy

When we speak of "green" in connection with the term "green energy," it represents a global strategy for social and economic development and a concern for the human living environment. Energy efficiency improvement, energy conservation, and CO_2 reduction are core elements of green energy. As a rapidly industrializing country, China's average annual GDP from 1980 to 2006 grew by around 9.9%, a remarkable achievement. During this period, China's energy requirements increased by around 131.6%.

Clean Energy Investments

As global concerns over climate change grow, China has been increasing its investments in clean energy to cut greenhouse gas emissions. The country has become a leader in several areas of renewable energy:

- **Solar Energy**: China is the world's largest market for solar water heaters, with 65 million square meters of solar water heaters sold in 2008. The widespread adoption of solar energy technology has significantly contributed to reducing carbon emissions.
- **Wind Power**: Plans to increase wind power capacity are also underway. China has surpassed the U.S. and Europe in the technology of reusable energy, becoming a global leader in wind power generation.

Government Initiatives

To support its commitment to renewable energy, the Chinese government has allocated 1.5-2% of government revenue in recent years to energy conservation, environmental protection, and technology development. These initiatives aim to promote sustainable development and address environmental challenges.

Sustainable Development Goals

China's approach to sustainable development involves integrating green energy into its national strategy. The government and the Chinese people recognize the importance of green energy in addressing issues related to people's livelihood, the environment, and the economy. The development of green energy is seen as a crucial step toward creating a sustainable future.

Conclusion

China's commitment to green energy and sustainable development highlights the country's dedication to environmental protection and economic growth. By investing in renewable energy and promoting energy efficiency, China is positioning itself as a leader in the global effort to combat climate change. These efforts are not only beneficial for the environment but also contribute to the long-term prosperity and well-being of the Chinese people.

31

CHAPTER 31: ARTIFICIAL INTELLIGENCE AND INNOVATION

Technological Progress and Innovation

China is a country that continues to welcome technological and scientific progress and innovation, and artificial intelligence (AI) is no exception. In 2017, China published more articles on deep learning than any other nation, making it the leading AI research country in this field, although it is slightly behind in overall AI research production. This demonstrates China's commitment to advancing AI and becoming a global leader in this cutting-edge technology.

New Generation AI Development Plan

Since the introduction of the 'New Generation AI Development Plan,' China has been focusing on AI fields that align with national interests. This ambitious plan aims to make China the world leader in AI by 2030, focusing on areas such as deep learning, cross-domain integration, and autonomous control. The plan emphasizes the importance of AI in driving economic growth, improving national security, and enhancing quality of life.

AI Research and Development

Chinese AI research is characterized by its rapid growth and increasing impact. The composition and origin of Chinese AI research have been examined by scientists within the country, revealing significant contributions to the global AI community. A dataset of Chinese AI self-citations supports claims of China's AI trophic shift, indicating a growing influence and leadership in AI research.

AI Surveillance Practice

One of the most critical and controversial aspects of AI deployment in China is its use in surveillance. This paper aims to critically examine and explore how and why AI surveillance practices are implemented in China. The country's positioning as a world AI leader has attracted significant criticism from the international community, particularly concerning privacy and human rights issues.

China has implemented extensive AI surveillance systems, such as the 'Sharp Eyes' program, which uses AI and facial recognition technology to monitor public spaces. These systems are designed to enhance public security and efficiency, but they have also raised concerns about the potential for abuse and the erosion of civil liberties.

Cultural and Technological Shifts

The ever-growing shifts in China's cultural and technological surroundings make it essential to study the high-profile criticism of its AI practices through a time-specific lens. As China continues to innovate and expand its AI capabilities, understanding the implications and consequences of these developments is crucial.

International Criticism and Ethical Concerns

The deployment of AI for surveillance in China has sparked a plethora of criticism from the international community. Ethical concerns regarding privacy, consent, and the potential misuse of AI technology are at the forefront of these debates. Critics argue that the extensive use of AI surveillance could lead to a dystopian society where individuals' freedoms and rights are severely restricted.

Future Directions and Implications

As China progresses in AI research and innovation, it is essential to balance technological advancements with ethical considerations. The future of AI in China will likely involve navigating these challenges while striving to achieve global leadership in AI. Continuous dialogue and collaboration with the international community will be vital in ensuring responsible and ethical AI development.

Conclusion

China's advancements in AI and its ambitious goals under the 'New Generation AI Development Plan' highlight the country's dedication to technological innovation. However, the use of AI for surveillance raises significant ethical concerns and criticism. Understanding and addressing these issues is crucial for the responsible development and deployment of AI technologies.

32

CHAPTER 32: CULTURAL DIPLOMACY: PROMOTING CHINESE

The Role of Cultural Diplomacy

Cultural diplomacy encompasses a rich and diverse range of interpretations, primarily focusing on intercultural relations and the role of cultural exchange in international relations. While a state's foreign policy often centers around tangible balances of power and military force, culture, arts, and non-violent persuasion play crucial roles in soft power strategies. These strategies aim to attract and engage global audiences rather than employing coercive tactics.

China's Cultural Rejuvenation

In recent years, China has projected its ongoing development and rejuvenation of culture not only within the global trade environment but also as the basis for its political appeal. This involves making Chinese culture more visible on the world stage through various festivals, exhibitions, and literature. Cultural diplomacy has become a key aspect of China's efforts to enhance its international image and influence.

Instruments of Cultural Diplomacy
Confucius Institutes and Language Schools

One of the most prominent tools of China's cultural diplomacy is the establishment of Confucius Institutes and Language Schools around the world. These institutions promote the Chinese language and culture through various activities, including:

- **Language Courses**: Teaching Mandarin to students of all ages and backgrounds.
- **Cultural Activities**: Hosting lectures, film screenings, tea ceremonies, and other cultural events.
- **Educational Exchange**: Facilitating academic exchanges and collaborations between Chinese and international institutions.

These efforts help to foster a deeper understanding and appreciation of Chinese culture globally.

Chinatowns

Chinese migration patterns to different regions of the world have led to the emergence of Chinatowns, which serve as cultural hubs showcasing Chinese traditions, cuisine, and festivals. Chinatowns are quintessential examples of sino-spatial diplomacy, highlighting the cultural element of China's global presence.

Media and Cultural Outreach

Chinese media and cultural productions also play a significant role in promoting Chinese culture internationally:

- **Television Stations**: Chinese television stations have been operating overseas, broadcasting Chinese news, dramas, and cultural programs to international audiences.
- **Films**: Traditional Chinese films, such as "The House of Flying Daggers," have garnered global attention and acclaim, bringing Chinese culture to a wider audience.

Economic and Tourism Impact

Cultural diplomacy has significant economic benefits, attracting larger numbers of tourists and contributing to local economies. The highly respected image that China enjoys today is bolstered by its cultural outreach efforts, making it a powerful force at a cultural level.

Conclusion

China's use of cultural diplomacy to promote its culture on the global stage highlights the importance of soft power in international relations. Through initiatives such as Confucius Institutes, Chinatowns, media outreach, and cultural productions, China has successfully enhanced its international image and influence. These efforts underscore the value of cultural exchange in fostering mutual understanding and global engagement.

33

CHAPTER 33: ECONOMIC BELT OF CHINA: YANGTZE RIVER

Historical and Cultural Context

China is vast, not just physically but also historically. Some of the earliest human ancestors have been found here. The country has experienced endless wars, power struggles, and invasions, with separate regions preferring independent governments. Chinese history deals not just with the rise and fall of empires but also with steady cooperation among various communities. It is a multi-layered tradition, with no single era standing out as the most important. China believes in the idea of continuity and ultimate integration of humanity, regardless of race, religion, and nationality.

Economic Development Plans

Various plans have been designed and drafted for China's economic outlook and technical development.

These plans aim to cope with different roads and policies for China's planned route toward 2030.

Belt and Road Initiative

The Belt and Road Initiative, launched in 2013, foresees investment in infrastructure along two major corridors:

1. **China-Europe (Nordic-Mediterranean Corridor)**: This corridor runs through Central Asia, the Middle East, and Russia.
2. **Land-Sea Route**: Connecting Indonesia, India, and Africa.

Focus on Yangtze River Delta and Pearl River Delta

Among these initiatives, the main focus of Chinese development priorities is the economic belt between the Yangtze River Delta and the Pearl River Delta.

Yangtze River Delta

The Yangtze River Delta, located in East China, is one of the most dynamic and economically prosperous regions in the country. Key cities in this delta include Shanghai, Nanjing, and Hangzhou. This region is known for its advanced manufacturing, financial services, and technology industries.

Pearl River Delta

The Pearl River Delta, situated in South China, is another vital economic hub. Key cities in this delta include Guangzhou, Shenzhen, and Hong Kong. This region is renowned for its innovation, technology, and international trade.

Development Strategies

The economic belt between these two deltas is governed by new development strategies that focus on:

- **Strategic Industries**: Promoting high-tech industries, advanced manufacturing, and green technology.
- **Infrastructure Development**: Building modern transportation networks, ports, and logistics hubs.
- **Educational and Industrial Bases**: Establishing world-class universities, research centers, and industrial parks to foster innovation and talent development.

Urbanization and Industrialization

Within China, increasing urbanization and industrialization, driven by improved transportation and modern ports, have led to significant migration from inner China to the southern regions. This migration supports the growth of the Yangtze and Pearl River Deltas, contributing to their economic development and integration into the global economy.

Conclusion

The economic belt of China, particularly the Yangtze River Delta and the Pearl River Delta, plays a crucial role in the country's economic growth and development. Through strategic planning and investment, China aims to enhance its infrastructure, promote innovation, and integrate its economy with global markets. These efforts reflect China's vision of continuity and integration, contributing to its overall prosperity and global influence.

34

CHAPTER 34: CHINESE PROVERBS AND FOLKLORE

Understanding Ancient Heritage Through Proverbs

Chinese proverbs in novels and other fiction act as a doorway to understanding ancient heritage. The traditional wisdom of the Chinese people has been preserved in the form of sayings that encapsulate the truth of various situations and have been handed down from generation to generation. These proverbs often feature metaphors and other figures of speech that have ties to Chinese folklore.

Cultural Significance of Proverbs

Chinese culture is highlighted in the use of these proverbs, and even when they are translated into English, the essence of the stories is preserved. Proverbs once served as teaching tools, much like Aesop's Fables. Just as stories of Robin Hood or Johnny Appleseed provide insight into American folklore, Chinese figures and stories offer a glimpse into Chinese culture. Many of China's most beloved sayings come from folklore, often explained through stories.

Xiaoshuo: A Genre of Chinese Literature

The genre known as "xiaoshuo" is one of the most popular forms of Chinese literature today. Xiaoshuo, which means "small talk," is generally written in a colloquial style and is easy to read. It is written both for entertainment and as a form of social criticism. This genre brings together various elements of Chinese history and culture, which often appear in modified form in the literature.

- **Characters**: Drawn from traditional opera, novels, or folklore.
- **Plots**: Often include struggles between good and evil, love and hatred, humor and sorrow.

Example: Dream of the Red Chamber

One of the best examples of xiaoshuo is "Dream of the Red Chamber." Written by Cao Xueqin in the late 18th century, this novel has been translated into German, Serbo-Croatian, Russian, Mongolian, Japanese, Czechoslovakian, and other languages. The novel weaves together various elements of Chinese culture, making it a valuable resource for understanding Chinese proverbs and folklore.

Conclusion

Chinese proverbs and folklore provide a rich tapestry of cultural heritage and traditional wisdom. Through genres like xiaoshuo and renowned works like "Dream of the Red Chamber," readers can gain a deeper understanding of the values, history, and stories that have shaped Chinese society over centuries.

35

CHAPTER 35: MARITIME SILK ROAD: HISTORICAL SIGNIFI

Historical Significance

In the long history of the Silk Road, the overland corridor of Central Asia is just one part. The Maritime Silk Road has an even longer history and has exerted a significant impact on the development of world politics, economy, culture, and trade between the East and West. The Maritime Silk Road, opened during the Qin and Han Dynasties, reached its peak of prosperity in the Tang and Song Dynasties. This maritime route extended over 30,000 miles through the sea areas of the South Pacific Ocean, Indian Ocean, Red Sea, and Mediterranean, crossing more than 20 countries and regions on all continents and forming a "Sea-China Road-Silk" trade circle. This route facilitated the exchange of Chinese pearls, silk, ceramics, tea, porcelain, paper, gunpowder, compasses, astronomical instruments, medicine, bronze mirrors, and China's four famous inventions.

Cultural and Trade Exchanges

The ancient Maritime Silk Road connected various exotic places of ancient China, including Fuzhou, Quanzhou, Guangzhou, Yangzhou, Hangzhou, and Ningbo. These ports served as vital hubs for trade and cultural exchange, allowing goods and ideas to flow between China and other civilizations. The route also reached places like Shiqu, Shanhou, Nizarm, Xiapo, Sanmiao, Houzhi, and Quruli, extending to Sibtipura, Koilani, Nirany, Yidanaya, Kollam, Amravati Idma, and beyond. This network of trade and cultural exchange helped to foster mutual understanding and cooperation among diverse cultures.

Contemporary Revival: 21st-Century Maritime Silk Road

China is now looking to the ancient Maritime Silk Road as a model to construct the 21st-Century Maritime Silk Road, aimed at developing cooperation on oceans with countries along the route. This initiative seeks to enhance economic ties, promote cultural exchange, and strengthen maritime cooperation. The first International Cooperation Summit was successfully held to advance these goals.

On October 12, 2013, at the end of a six-day inspection tour of the ancient Maritime Silk Road, Indian Ambassador Ashok Kantha remarked that the ancient route abolished barriers of mountains and rivers and became an important bond connecting Chinese and Indian civilizations. China is willing, and India can join together to inherit and carry forward the friendship and cultural exchange left by the ancient Maritime Silk Road as a contribution to friendship, harmony, and development between the two countries.

Conclusion

The Maritime Silk Road holds a profound historical significance, having played a crucial role in the development of global trade, culture, and politics. Its contemporary revival as the 21st-Century Maritime Silk Road aims to build on this rich heritage, fostering cooperation and connectivity among nations. This initiative underscores the enduring importance of the Maritime Silk Road in promoting mutual understanding and global development.

36

CHAPTER 36: CHINESE TEA CULTURE: HISTORY, VARIETIE

The Birthplace of Tea

China is the birthplace of tea and the homeland of tea culture. Chinese tea culture has a long history and reflects the great achievements of the Chinese nation in the development and utilization of nature. With more than 1,000 varieties and styles, China boasts the most types of tea in the world. Each style of tea has its own unique characteristics and can be said to have its own personality.

The Role of Tea in Contemporary Society

In today's China, tea plays a role beyond merely arousing the palate. For the vast majority of people, tea has found a place in their hearts. While it may not be considered essential, it is definitely a luxury—a small intoxicant that provides a respite between leisure and fatigue. The pursuit of tea is one way of understanding the spirit of contemporary society.

Aesthetic Value and Cultural Expression

Tea holds a much higher aesthetic value and cultural expression than a simple beverage. Throughout Chinese history, tea has been celebrated in legends, poems, and quotations that reflect every aspect of Eastern culture. Tea is not only important in Chinese etiquette but also represents a popular spiritual existence that transcends mere sensual satisfaction.

Propagation of Tea Culture

Propagating the elegance, fresh air, and health benefits of tea has become a strong selling point for China in foreign countries. The habit of drinking tea elevates the trivial and ordinary into a form of consciousness and initiative. Even in busy modern life, many people have joined the group of tea lovers, happily flowing in and out of the world of tea.

Varieties of Chinese Tea

China's tea varieties are vast and diverse, each with its own unique flavor profile and preparation method. Some of the most well-known types include:

- **Green Tea**: Known for its fresh and light flavor, green tea is minimally processed and retains most of its natural antioxidants.
- **Black Tea**: Fully oxidized, black tea has a rich and robust flavor. It is often enjoyed with milk or sugar.
- **Oolong Tea**: A partially oxidized tea that combines the qualities of both green and black tea.

Oolong tea is known for its complex and aromatic profile.
- **White Tea**: Made from young tea leaves and buds, white tea is minimally processed and has a delicate and subtle flavor.
- **Pu-erh Tea**: A fermented tea that improves with age, pu-erh has a deep, earthy flavor and is often consumed for its health benefits.

Tea Rituals and Etiquette

Chinese tea rituals and etiquette reflect the cultural significance of tea. Traditional tea ceremonies emphasize mindfulness, respect, and harmony. Key elements of a tea ceremony include:

- **Preparation**: Carefully selecting and preparing the tea leaves, water, and utensils.
- **Brewing**: The method of brewing varies depending on the type of tea, but it often involves multiple infusions to fully appreciate the flavor.
- **Serving**: Pouring the tea with grace and precision, often using small, elegant cups.
- **Enjoyment**: Savoring the tea's aroma, taste, and appearance, and appreciating the moment of tranquility.

Conclusion

Chinese tea culture is a rich and multifaceted tradition that encompasses history, varieties, and rituals. From its origins in ancient China to its place in modern society, tea continues to be a symbol of elegance, health, and cultural expression. Understanding and experiencing Chinese tea culture offers a unique window into the soul of China.

37

CHAPTER 37: PANDA CONSERVATION AND ECOTOURISM IN C

Habitat and Conservation Status

In the wild, pandas can only be found in China, and their population is limited to a few fragmented habitat patches in the mountain ranges of Sichuan, Gansu, and Shaanxi provinces. This limited distribution has led to the giant panda's status as a global flagship species for conservation. Since the 1960s, China has conducted simultaneous field and zoo research on pandas, leading to valuable insights into their biology, ecology, genetics, and reproduction.

Conservation Efforts and Protected Areas

To better protect this endangered species, the Chinese government has established a network of protected areas that include nature reserves, parks, and other protected zones. These areas also feature live panda exhibits set up in the habitats of wild giant pandas. These enclosures, filled with wet bamboo, serve not only as conservation sites but also as tourist destinations, offering the public and international visitors a unique opportunity for ecotourism.

The China Conservation and Research Center for the Giant Panda houses the most intact captive panda territories, accounting for two-thirds of the world's captive panda population and over 40 years of management experience. Older centers such as those in Chengdu, Chongqing Wu, and Beijing Zoo also play significant roles in panda conservation.

Challenges in Panda Breeding

Panda breeding has a history of nearly 50 years, beginning with China's first breeding facility at the Beijing Zoo in 1963. Research has played a key role in panda conservation, but breeding captive pandas remains challenging. These bears experience a physiological change each year for potential reproductive mating, and the estrus cycle of the female occurs only once per year for a little more than two days. This brief window makes successful mating between female and male pandas very difficult, with few copulations observed in the wild.

Ecotourism and Public Engagement

The establishment of panda reserves and breeding centers has not only aided in conservation but also promoted ecotourism. Locations like the Chengdu Research Base of Giant Panda Breeding attract thousands of visitors annually, raising awareness and generating funds for conservation efforts. Ecotourism initiatives aim to educate the public about panda conservation while providing an engaging and memorable experience.

Conclusion

Panda conservation in China combines scientific research, habitat protection, and public engagement through ecotourism. The challenges of breeding and maintaining captive panda populations highlight the importance of continued efforts and innovation in conservation strategies. By protecting this iconic species and promoting sustainable tourism, China is working to ensure the survival of the giant panda for future generations.

38

CHAPTER 38: CHINESE POETRY: CLASSICAL VERSES AND M

The Timeless Beauty of Chinese Poetry

Poets across the world often respond to similar conditions or emotions, yet Chinese poetry, with its extensive history, holds unique characteristics and a distinct attraction for readers. Chinese poetry inspires reflection on the natural and human worlds, ways of living, and despair, beckoning readers to dive into both ancient heritage and modern wonders.

Classical Verses

Origins and Early Works

In China, the earliest writings, including poetry, are found in the inscriptions on oracle bones and tortoise shells from the Shang Dynasty. One of the most significant early collections is the **Shijing (Classic of Poetry)**, believed to have been composed during the Western Zhou and early Eastern Zhou periods. Confucius is credited with editing and compiling the Shijing, teaching his disciples to appreciate poetry for its ideas and literary beauty.

Characteristics of Classical Chinese Poetry

Classical Chinese poetry is known for its refined language, intricate structures, and deep philosophical reflections. Common themes include nature, love, friendship, and the fleeting nature of life. Famous poets like **Li Bai**, **Du Fu**, and **Wang Wei** have left an indelible mark on Chinese literature with their timeless verses.

Modern Poets

The Rise of Contemporary Chinese Poetry

Aside from traditional Chinese poetry, the last century has seen a surge in interest in contemporary Chinese poetry. Scholars like Tingting Tan have furthered the work of earlier researchers by undertaking comprehensive analyses of modern Chinese poetry. Notable works include **The Approaching of the Last Steamer: Modern Poetry in China (1899–1949)** and **Chinese Modern Poetry in the Age of Science (1900–2000)**.

Discrepancies and Evaluations

Despite frequent written discussions on contemporary Chinese poetry in English, a serious discrepancy in poetic evaluation persists, limiting our understanding and appreciation. Regular assessment of modern poets is crucial for bridging this gap. Eminent sinologists have contributed articles shedding light on different poets, their writings, significant poetic movements, and the evolution of modern poetry in China.

Notable Modern Poets and Movements

Modern Chinese poets have continued to innovate while drawing from the rich traditions of their predecessors. Some notable modern poets include **Ai Qing**, **Bei Dao**, and **Xi Chuan**. Their works explore themes of identity, social change, and existentialism, reflecting the complexities of contemporary Chinese society.

Conclusion

Chinese poetry, both classical and modern, offers a rich tapestry of literary beauty and profound reflections. From the earliest inscriptions to the latest poetic innovations, Chinese poets have continuously enriched the cultural heritage of their nation. By exploring classical verses and modern poets, readers can gain a deeper appreciation of the timeless and evolving nature of Chinese poetry.

39

CHAPTER 39: DIGITAL REVOLUTION AND E-COMMERCE IN C

The Rise of E-Commerce

The latter half of 1993 marks the first time the word e-commerce officially appeared. Over the subsequent quarter-century, four digital giants emerged from relative obscurity and indelibly shaped the modern world: Amazon, Alphabet, Microsoft, and Apple. One might well ask how China is not part of this list. Indeed, the country boasts major coups with Alibaba, Tencent, Baidu, Didi Chuxing, and Xiaomi, all of which dominate global sectors or at least rank among the top three.

Jack Ma and the Birth of Alibaba

In 1997, ex-English teacher Jack Ma traveled to the United States and was introduced to the Internet, an experience that was life-changing. Today, Jack Ma is China's e-commerce guru and founder of Alibaba, the world's fourth most valuable Internet company. Alibaba has played a pivotal role in transforming China's retail landscape and setting global trends in e-commerce.

Digital Giants Transforming China's Economy

Companies such as Alibaba and Huawei are helping to transform China into an innovation economy. According to a PwC report, China is set to become "the engine for global digital technology." The digital tsunami is not only reorienting China's internal economic structure but also influencing how Chinese consumers behave. Key developments include:

- **Mobile Payment Apps**: Platforms like WeChat Pay and Alipay have revolutionized payment methods, making transactions quick and seamless.
- **Online Shopping**: E-commerce platforms like Taobao and JD.com have transformed retail, offering consumers a vast array of products at their fingertips.

Leading the World in E-Commerce

China today leads the world in e-commerce by a considerable margin. E-commerce is no longer just one aspect of the retail industry. According to the PwC report, integrated technologies are enablers of retail disruption. As the retail ecosystem has developed, integrating several functions from media to payment to service, digital retail has become much bigger and harder to define.

Impact on Consumer Behavior

The rise of digital platforms has significantly impacted Chinese consumer behavior:

- **Convenience**: The ability to shop online anytime and anywhere has driven a surge in e-commerce activities.
- **Diverse Choices**: Consumers have access to a wide range of products from local and international brands.
- **Personalized Shopping**: Advanced algorithms and data analytics provide personalized recommendations, enhancing the shopping experience.

Conclusion

The digital revolution and e-commerce boom in China have reshaped the country's economic landscape and influenced global trends. As digital giants like Alibaba, Tencent, and Huawei continue to innovate, China's position as a leader in e-commerce and digital technology is set to strengthen. The integration of digital technologies into everyday life underscores the transformative power of the digital revolution in shaping modern society.

40

CHAPTER 40: TRADITIONAL CHINESE FESTIVALS: LUNAR N

Introduction

Chinese culture and traditions are as diverse as its people and language, and there are numerous unique customs, celebrations, and practices that foreign tourists encounter for the first time in China. Three of the most important traditional Chinese festivals—Lunar New Year, Mid-Autumn Festival, and Dragon Boat Festival—offer a feast of color, sound, and taste. Let's delve into the details of these lively events.

Lunar New Year (Spring Festival)

Lunar New Year, also known as the Spring Festival, is China's most important festival. Celebrations last for 15 days and are marked by feasts, firecrackers, family gatherings, and other traditional customs. The festival usually begins on the first day of the lunar calendar and culminates with the Lantern Festival.

- **Family Reunions**: At night, families often come together from far and near to reunite. Every family member holds a plate of snacks and fruits, waiting for midnight to bring happiness and luck.
- **Festivities**: The Spring Festival features a huge number of people, both locals and international visitors, who spend the festival in China. Tiananmen Square and two televisions on both sides broadcast live pageant performances throughout the week-long holiday, which millions of viewers enjoy with enthusiasm.
- **Firecrackers and Performances**: The sound of firecrackers, temple gongs, and bells fills the air to drive off evil spirits and entertain people. Firecrackers represent happiness and are used both in the countryside and cities, creating a lively and festive atmosphere.

Mid-Autumn Festival

The Mid-Autumn Festival, also known as the Moon Festival, is celebrated on the 15th day of the 8th month of the lunar calendar. This festival is dedicated to the moon and is a time for family reunions and thanksgiving.

- **Mooncakes**: Mooncakes, a traditional pastry filled with sweet or savory ingredients, are an essential part of the Mid-Autumn Festival. They are shared among family members and symbolize reunion and togetherness.

- **Moon Gazing**: Families gather to appreciate the full moon, which is believed to be at its brightest and roundest on this night. The moon is a symbol of harmony and unity.
- **Lanterns and Performances**: Lantern displays and cultural performances are common during the festival. People create and light lanterns, which are often released into the sky or floated on water.

Dragon Boat Festival

The Dragon Boat Festival, also known as Duanwu Festival, is celebrated on the 5th day of the 5th month of the lunar calendar. This festival commemorates the ancient poet Qu Yuan and is characterized by dragon boat races and the consumption of zongzi (rice dumplings).

- **Dragon Boat Races**: Colorful dragon boat races are the highlight of the festival. Teams paddle in unison to the beat of drums, competing to reach the finish line first.
- **Zongzi**: Zongzi, sticky rice dumplings wrapped in bamboo leaves, are traditionally eaten during the Dragon Boat Festival. They are often filled with sweet or savory ingredients and symbolize the rice offerings thrown into the river to honor Qu Yuan.
- **Cultural Activities**: Various cultural activities, including performances and rituals, are held to celebrate the festival and preserve its traditions.

Conclusion

Traditional Chinese festivals like Lunar New Year, Mid-Autumn Festival, and Dragon Boat Festival offer a rich and immersive experience of China's cultural heritage. These festivals bring together family, friends, and communities in celebration, creating memories that last a lifetime. Whether through the vibrant parades of the Spring Festival, the serene moon gazing of the Mid-Autumn Festival, or the thrilling dragon boat races, these events showcase the essence of Chinese traditions and customs.

41

CHAPTER 41: CHINESE DANCE AND PERFORMING ARTS: CLA

The Essence of Chinese Dance and Performing Arts

Chinese dance and performing arts are the embodiment of Chinese people's spiritual and artistic pursuit. The richness, elegance, simplicity, and beauty of these arts reflect the essence of human life. From picturesque classical forms to bold and vibrant contemporary productions, China's dance and performing arts continue to evolve, keeping ancient traditions alive while embracing modern innovation.

Early Origins and Rituals

The origins of Chinese dance lie in ancient rituals throughout East Asia. Since the earliest times of Chinese civilization, important events such as birth, marriage, and harvest were celebrated with dance. Early forms of folk dance, often performed in circles, symbolized communal celebration and unity.

Dance in Chinese Opera

Dance in Chinese opera is known as "xi" (Chinese: ◇; pinyin: xì; literally: 'drama'). In Chinese opera, dances are integrated into the narrative and simple dialogues of selected scenes. These dances evolved into highly structured activities that combine comic and dramatic effects. Unlike the rich, dramatic styles of European opera, Chinese opera developed its unique artistic expression with minimal outside influence.

Government Support and Cultural Exchange

The Chinese government has always attached great importance to dance and performing arts. National awards have been given to various dance and acting projects, and artistic troupes often participate in cultural exchange performances with foreign countries. Performing arts have traditionally received priority in China's cultural policies, highlighting their significance in promoting cultural heritage and national identity.

Classical Dance Forms

Traditional Chinese Dance

Traditional Chinese dance encompasses a wide range of styles, including:

- **Classical Dance**: Inspired by ancient Chinese art, poetry, and literature, classical dance is characterized by its graceful movements and intricate techniques.
- **Ethnic Folk Dance**: Each ethnic group in China has its unique dance traditions, reflecting their

cultural heritage and way of life. Examples include Tibetan, Mongolian, and Uighur dances.

Contemporary Dance and Innovation

Contemporary Chinese dance blends traditional elements with modern techniques, creating innovative and dynamic performances. Modern productions often incorporate contemporary themes and experimental styles, pushing the boundaries of dance and performing arts.

Influential Contemporary Dance Companies

- **Beijing Dance Academy**: One of the leading institutions for dance education in China, renowned for its rigorous training and exceptional performances.
- **Tao Dance Theater**: A contemporary dance company known for its minimalist and avant-garde choreography, gaining international acclaim.

Solo Performances and Musical Excellence

China maintains a particularly strong tradition of solo performances, especially in concert piano. Chinese musicians have achieved global recognition for their technical prowess and artistic expression, contributing to the world's musical landscape.

Conclusion

Chinese dance and performing arts represent a rich tapestry of tradition and innovation. From early ritual dances to contemporary productions, these arts continue to evolve while preserving their cultural heritage.

The support of the Chinese government and the dedication of artists ensure that China's performing arts remain vibrant and influential on the global stage.

42

CHAPTER 42: FUTURE OF CHINA: CHALLENGES AND OPPORT

Esteemed Institutions and Thought Leadership

Tsinghua University stands as one of China's most esteemed educational institutions, having produced many of the country's and region's current political, business, military, and thought leaders. Consistently ranked highly, often number one in Asia, Tsinghua University embodies the pinnacle of academic excellence. Being chosen to attend the first "Tsinghua International Symposium: Ancient Heritage of China, Modern China" and present this address is indeed a great honor.

Ancient Heritage and Modern Growth

China's ancient heritage dates back to at least the Neolithic period, with evidence for the existence of Homo sapiens around 40,800 years ago, and a rich history spanning over 3,500 years. This deep historical foundation lays the groundwork for understanding China's current status as an economic and political power that has been growing exponentially for the last 40 years.

Challenges and Opportunities

Despite its impressive growth, China faces numerous challenges as it moves further into the 21st century:

Social Challenges

- **Aging Population**: China is grappling with an aging population and a shrinking workforce, which could impact economic growth and social stability.
- **Urbanization**: Rapid urbanization brings challenges such as housing shortages, infrastructure demands, and environmental degradation.

Economic Challenges

- **Economic Transition**: Transitioning from a manufacturing-based economy to a service and innovation-driven economy presents both opportunities and challenges.
- **Trade Relations**: Navigating complex trade relations and tariffs, particularly with major economies like the United States, requires careful diplomacy and strategy.

Environmental Challenges

- **Pollution**: Air and water pollution remain significant concerns, impacting public health and the environment.
- **Climate Change**: Addressing climate change through sustainable practices and green energy initiatives is crucial for China's long-term environmental health.

Political Challenges

- **Governance**: Balancing strong centralized control with the need for greater transparency and rule of law is a delicate act.
- **International Relations**: Maintaining a peaceful yet assertive global presence involves navigating geopolitical tensions and fostering international cooperation.

Opportunities for Growth

- **Innovation and Technology**: China is poised to become a global leader in technology and innovation, with significant investments in AI, renewable energy, and infrastructure.
- **Belt and Road Initiative**: This ambitious initiative aims to strengthen trade and economic ties across Asia, Europe, and Africa, creating new opportunities for growth and cooperation.
- **Cultural Diplomacy**: Promoting Chinese culture globally through soft power strategies enhances China's international image and influence.

Sustaining Growth and Ethical Considerations

The key questions to be asked are: Can China's growth be sustained indefinitely? Will this growth adhere to established ethics, norms, and values? These are critical considerations as China continues to expand its global influence.

Conclusion

China's increasing, high-profile, and peaceful yet sometimes bellicose global presence represents both its greatest opportunity and challenge in the 21st century. As China navigates social, economic, environmental, and political challenges, it must also seize opportunities for innovation, cooperation, and cultural exchange. The path forward requires a balance of growth and ethical governance to ensure a prosperous and stable future.